# Tales of Prime Ministers in Ancient China

*Compiled and Translated by* Cheng Yu

**Foreign Languages Press**  Beijing

First Edition    2001

Home Page:
  http://www.flp.com.cn
E-mail Addresses:
  info@flp.com.cn
  sales@flp.com.cn

ISBN 7-119-02917-7
© Foreign Languages Press, Beijing, China, 2001

Published by Foreign Languages Press
24 Baiwanzhuang Road, Beijing 100037, China

Printed by Beijing Foreign Languages Printing House
19 Chegongzhuang Xilu, Beijing 100044, China

Distributed by China International Book Trading Corporation
35 Chegongzhuang Xilu, Beijing 100044, China
P.O. Box 399, Beijing, China

*Printed in the People's Republic of China*

# Foreword

Prime ministers are not rare on today's international political stage, yet the prime ministers of ancient China perhaps tell a different tale.

Through the Shang Dynasty of over three thousand years ago to the Qing Dynasty of not even a century past, hundreds of Chinese prime ministers rose and fell. And throughout these ages, although the names of the prime ministers may have changed, the momentous role they all played remained much the same: the number one administrator in the country. They were, after all, selected by absolute rulers, and thus also were their destinies controlled by these overlords. Therefore, however talented and powerful they might have been, they ultimately could never be their own masters. This may be the most significant difference between those prime ministers of ancient China and those of today.

The clever and the cruel, the loyal and the deceiving, the efficient and the inept: prime ministers of all such descriptions take their place in the long history that formed China. As the highest-ranking administrator, a prime minister had only one individual over him yet he had millions of people under him. Thus a prime minister could powerfully influence the court, thereby not just changing the course of history but also defining the age for all time. All of this notwithstanding, in a feudal society it was the supreme ruler who determined the life and death of all subjects, including the prime minister. As the ancient Chinese saying goes: "To consort with a king is tantamount to living with a tiger." To be a prime minister at certain times was to occupy a most precarious position—which is no doubt why many a prime minister in ancient China did not die of natural causes.

The 30 prime ministers in this book span almost all of the dynasties of Chinese history. Those selected, from among the hundreds more, were chosen for their being representative of their time. Many of their stories are a part of the common heritage of China even to this day; and their achievements and failings, their rights and their wrongs, have been and will be discussed forever.

# CONTENTS

## Shang Dynasty (*c.* 16th-11th century BC)
Yi Yin, the First Prime Minister Recorded in Chinese History … 2

## Western Zhou Dynasty (*c.* 11th century –770 BC)
Jiang Shang, Prime Minister of Legend … 10

## Spring and Autumn Period (770-476 BC)
Guan Zhong, Who Made His Ruler the Overlord of All States … 18
Yan Ying, the Diminutive Yet Eloquent Prime Minister … 26
Wu Zixu, Whose Hair Turned White Overnight … 33
Fan Li, Prime Minister to a Titan … 43
Shang Yang, the Great Reformer … 53

## Warring States Period (475-221 BC)
Su Qin, Prime Minister of Six States … 63
Lord Mengchang the Hospitable … 71

| | |
|---|---|
| Zou Ji, Music Maestro and Fine Prime Minister | 79 |
| Lü Buwei, More Speculator Than Prime Minister | 87 |

## Qin Dynasty (221-206 BC)
| | |
|---|---|
| Li Si, the First Prime Minister of a Unifiied China | 99 |

## Han Dynasty (206 BC-220 AD)
| | |
|---|---|
| Xiao He, Who Helped Liu Bang Establish the Han Dynasty | 109 |
| Cao Cao, Statesman, Strategist and Poet All in One | 118 |

## Three Kingdoms Period (220-265)
| | |
|---|---|
| Zhuge Liang the Mastermind | 133 |

## Jin Dynasty (265-420)
| | |
|---|---|
| Xie An, a Remarkable High-born Prime Minister | 151 |

## Southern and Northern Dynasties (420-589)
| | |
|---|---|
| Cui Hao, Han Scholar-Prime Minister for a Xianbei Kingdom | 156 |

## Sui Dynasty (581-618)
| | |
|---|---|
| Gao Jiong, Henchman of Sui Dynasty's Emperor Wendi | 160 |

## Tang Dynasty (618-907)
Wei Zheng, Mirror for the Emperor — 165
Fang Xuanling, Most Capable Aide to Emperor Taizong — 175
Di Renjie, Prime Minister to the Only Female Emperor — 183

## Five Dynasties (907-960)
Feng Dao, Rolling Through Troubled Times — 193

## Song Dynasty (960-1279)
Sima Guang, Conservative in Politics and Reformer in Historiography — 198
Wang Anshi, Illustrious Statesman and Man of Letters — 208
Cai Jing, Great Calligrapher, Bad Prime Minister — 214
Qin Hui's Thousand-Year Evil Name — 220

## Yuan Dynasty (1271-1368)
Yelü Chucai, Distinguished Statesman from the Qidan — 230

## Ming Dynasty (1368-1644)
Shi Kefa, a Loyal Prime Minister to a Doomed Dynasty — 235

## Qing Dynasty (1644-1911)
Dorgon, the Iron-handed Prince Regent    242
He Shen, the Most Corrupt Prime Minister in Chinese History    252

# Shang Dynasty
# (c.16 th-11th century BC)

# Yi Yin, the First Prime Minister Recorded in Chinese History

Who was the very first prime minister in China? No one knows. The Chinese people of five thousand years ago left no records about their prime ministers. Even if they had, no traces have yet been found. Fortunately, in the later years of the Qing Dynasty, peasants in present-day Henan Province unearthed some bones and tortoise shells inscribed with an unusual calligraphy. It was established later that these characters dated way back to the Shang Dynasty (*c.* 16th-11th century BC).

From these deciphered artifacts, researchers deduced that a man by the name of Yi Yin was the first prime minister of the Shang Dynasty, making him the earliest recorded prime minister in Chinese history during the 16th century BC.

The tale of Yi Yin's birth makes for fascinating legend. It is recounted that in the latter years of the Xia Dynasty (which preceded the Shang), a young lady in Shen, a vassal state of the Xia empire, one day found a naked baby lying under a large tree. The girl presented the baby to the ruler, who then ordered his cooks to raise this child.

Yi Yin grew up to become a celebrated chef. There is a saying in China that goes: "Running a country is like cooking a banquet." Yi Yin's story might best exemplify this famous aphorism.

When the ruler found Yi Yin to be a person of talent, he employed him as his daughter's teacher. Even though he lived within the palace, Yi Yin made a point of carefully observing the developments beyond the palace walls. He soon discovered that the ruler of the Xia Dynasty, Jie, was a tyrant detested by people all over the country. This made Yi Yin resolve to assist a virtuous ruler to eliminate the Xia so as to establish a more just dynasty.

Yi Yin's renown meanwhile had spread to the neighboring vassal state of Shang, whose ruler, Tang, asked the ruler of Shen to send this personage to him. The ruler of Shen, however, rejected Tang's request, and Yi Yin was forced to bide his time.

One day, Yi Yin learned that Tang was betrothed to the daughter of the ruler of Shen. He beseeched the Shen ruler to let him go to the State of Shang as a part of his daughter's dowry, as a kind of bonded slave. This time the ruler of

Shen allowed him to go.

Having heard of Yi Yin as an excellent chef, Tang let Yi Yin prepare his meals in the Shang palace each day. Thus, taking every meal as an opportunity to sound his ideas, Yi Yin described the prevailing political situation and convinced Tang that he should replace the unjust Jie. Being a chef, Yi Yin compared affairs of state to the art of cooking. It was not long before Tang realized that Yi Yin possessed exceptional ability. He pronounced Yi Yin to be freed from his bondage, and appointed him his most senior minister.

Under Yi Yin's steady guidance, the State of Shang grew stronger day by day. However, Tang grew worried that Jie's overweening ambitions could endanger his own state before he could act. He sent Yi Yin to Jie's palace to find out the actual situation in the Xia empire.

Jie, on his part, had also grown fearful of the expanding power and territory of the State of Shang, so he confronted Yi Yin in his court. The astute Yi Yin calmed Jie and won his trust. Beyond this, Jie was not too interested in affairs of state at all. His main objective was to delight in a life of luxury. Fine wines and beautiful women were all he needed. So as to divert any suspicions, as well as to entice Jie, Yi Yin presented him with two beautiful women.

Yi Yin remained in Xia for three years carefully studying Jie's rule. Having learned what he wished to know, he felt it time to return to Shang.

Tang strongly felt they should attack Xia immediately, after hearing Yi Yin's report. Yi Yin, however, thought this premature since Xia's strength was still greater than that of Shang. He instead advised Tang not to pay tribute to Xia in the coming year, for the purpose of flying Jie's kite.

When he heard that Tang would not pay tribute, Jie was enraged. He gathered together troops from nine states and marched on the capital city of Shang. Yi Yin then told Tang: "The facts tell us that the Xia Dynasty still holds power and appeal. Sire, acknowledge your mistake and ask for punishment." Whereupon Tang went himself to see Jie.

The moment Tang arrived at the capital city of Xia, Jie had Tang arrested. But Yi Yin had already calculated on this. On the one hand, he presented Jie enormous riches from the treasury as well as the most beautiful women of the land, and on the other hand, he bribed the more cunning officials of Xia. Jie was delighted when he obtained so many treasures from Shang, and he soon ordered that Tang be freed.

Tang and Yi Yin then plotted to eliminate Xia's principal allied states one by one. After several battles, Shang achieved this objective, and the balance of power soon shifted between Xia and Shang.

Yi Yin then said to Tang, "Sire, do not pay tribute this year, then just wait and watch."

As soon as Jie heard the news, he again called for troops from his allied states. This time nobody obeyed him. Jie, it seemed, had dissipated most of his support. Yi Yin then told Tang, "The time is ripe to attack Xia."

In the year 1711 BC, Shang and Xia fought a decisive battle in the wilds of Mingtiao. This was a one-sided war: Xia soldiers did not want to sacrifice their lives for an unjust Jie, while Shang troops advanced courageously. Jie had lost this war from the very outset. In the end, Jie was captured by Tang, and died three years later.

After the Mingtiao battle, Shang troops lost no time occupying the capital city of Xia. Pacifying the officials and common people of Xia, Tang declared the eradication of the Xia Dynasty and the establishment of the Shang Dynasty.

After Tang witnessed how the Xia Dynasty had fallen, in order not to repeat Xia's mistake, he instituted policies opposite to Xia's. His kindness to vassal state rulers and the common people led to a stable society.

As Tang's prime minister, Yi Yin was the most suitable adviser and administrator of Tang's policy of benevolence.

Tang died after 13 years as the ruler of the Shang Dynasty, and as his first son had died even earlier, it fell to the second son to ascend the throne. However, this son also died after two years. Yi Yin then helped Tang's youngest son become king. It seemed that Tang's sons were all to die young, and this one was to be no exception. He died four years later, and it became the turn of the next generation. Thus it was that Tang's first grandson, Tai Jia, ascended the throne.

Through the exertions of the three rulers before Tai Jia, Shang had developed into a stable country with greater and greater grain harvests. Unfortunately, Tai Jia, unlike his grandfather and father, was not familiar with the failings of the Xia Dynasty. Like Jie, he too slipped into a decadent lifestyle and ignored national affairs. Tai Jia also arbitrarily punished or even killed any officials who disobeyed his orders.

At first, Yi Yin tried his best to teach Tai Jia, relating him stories about Xia's downfall and

Tang's policy of benevolence. However, faithful admonitions being unpleasant to his ears, Tai Jia began to suspect Yi Yin of plotting to take over the throne. Yi Yin then quickly went into action for the sake of the Shang Dynasty. He had Tai Jia arrested and imprisoned in a suburban palace —a famous historical incident in Chinese history.

After three years, Tai Jia realized the errors of his ways, and promised to repent and start anew. Yi Yin then welcomed Tai Jia back into his old palace and returned him to power. No longer his errant self, Tai Jia behaved as Tang had done before him, practicing a policy of benevolence. Yi Yin too was glad to witness this transformation, and documented what happened to Tai Jia.

After Tai Jia, his son Wo Ding became the ruler of Shang. From Tang to Wo Ding, the ruler of Shang was changed four times, and it seemed as if Yi Yin would be the eternal prime minister of Shang. A personage gifted with longevity, Yi Yin assisted five rulers, and it is said that Yi Yin died at the age of 100. He was given a burial befitting a king and Wo Ding observed mourning beside Yi Yin's grave for three whole years.

# Western Zhou Dynasty
(*c.* 11th century-770 BC)

# Jiang Shang, Prime Minister of Legend

In the late Shang Dynasty (11th century BC), the leader of the vassal state Zhou, historically known as King Wen of Zhou, visited the State of Zang. There, it is said, he came upon an old man fishing in the Weishui River. Strangely enough, the fisherman was using neither bait nor hook. "This must indeed be a most extraordinary person," King Wen concluded, "one who does not care for loss or gain, but yearns for freedom." King Wen felt he should appoint such an unusual character to govern the state, yet he was worried that such an action would upset his ministers, uncles and cousins. The next morning he summoned his court, and said, "Last night I dreamed I saw a man of character, bearded, with a dark complexion, riding a dappled horse, half of whose hooves were red. This man said to me: 'Pass your government to the worthy of Zang, and your people shall escape calamity.'"

His ministers replied with one voice: "The late king, Ji Li! That's who that was. He too had a dark complexion and a beard. And he liked to ride a dappled horse with red hooves. It must have been him you dreamed of."

King Wen replied, "Perhaps you are right. Let us ask the diviner."

But a minister cautioned, "It is the command of the late king. Your Majesty should not doubt this. There is no need for a diviner."

"Very well," agreed the King.

And this is how, it is said, King Wen handed over the government to the Old Man of Zang.

That this story, as related above, is pure legend, there is no doubt. The Old Man of Zang, was in reality Lü Shang, also known as "Master Jiang" to later generations.

Since Yu, the great legendary king of ancient times, had conferred the territory of Lü upon Jiang Shang's ancestors, Jiang Shang was also known as Lü Shang.

As a man of unparalleled talent, Jiang Shang had earlier found no opportunity to put his sound ideas into practice, so he had wandered from one place to another throughout the best years of his life. It is said that he was very poor in his youth. So much so that when his wife cast him out of the house, he had to find work as a butcher in the market. He is said to have tried his hand at many jobs, but in the end failed at all of them. His energy exhausted, he had come to the Weishui River to make a living, catching fish. However, he had still hoped to one day meet a virtuous ruler who would finally employ his genius fully.

Many years had passed, and while his black hair turned white, his virtuous ruler still did not appear. Just as it seemed that Jiang Shang would pass life by as a fisherman, King Wen of Zhou had come by the Weishui River and discovered him.

At first, the king appointed Jiang Shang as only a petty official in Guanyun so as to test him. After one year, he had managed the region so judiciously that, it is said, even the wind there obeyed him. One night, King Wen dreamed of a most beautiful woman who came crying to him. When the king asked her what was wrong, she replied: "I am the daughter of the God of Mount Taishan, and my husband is the God of the Eastern Sea. I am now on my way home. As always, wherever I travel, heavy winds and rains accompany me. Today I have to pass through Guanyun to go home. But if I do, the good reputation of the official in Guanyun may be damaged. I am truly in a dilemma."

When the king woke up, he sent for Jiang Shang and asked him to explain his dream. As

Jiang Shang was saying he did not know how to explain it, someone reported that heavy winds and rains were hitting Guanyun. From that time onward, the king, awed by Jiang Shang's honesty as well as his power to gain the sympathy of even the deities, handed over the reins of government to Jiang Shang.

Under Jiang Shang, traditional order was maintained and arbitrary new laws were not issued. Three years later, as King Wen toured his realm, he found that the chiefs of the departments no longer abused their positions, and that no illegal weights or measures had entered the country. Peace and tranquillity were to be found everywhere.

After King Wen died, his son King Wu ascended the throne. The new ruler honored Jiang Shang as "Shi Shang Fu," the equivalent of prime minister.

The ruling king in the final years of the Shang Dynasty was known as an unprincipled profligate. King Wen and King Wu had both dreamed of eliminating this corrupt and decadent government so as to build a new dynasty of their own. That too was Jiang Shang's dream. However, while the Shang Dynasty was still powerful and more than a match for Zhou, King

Wu and Jiang Shang had to bide their time.

Bo Yi and Shu Qi were two princes of another vassal state, who, having relinquished the throne after their father's death, had come to Zhou a few years earlier since they believed King Wen to be a wise ruler. When they had heard his son, King Wu, wanted to attack Shang, they opposed and reproached him: "You are a subject of Shang. Is it right for you to attack your sovereign?"

When some guards laid their weapons on the heads of the brothers, Jiang Shang intervened and told them to withdraw: "As subjects of Shang, they are loyal to their sovereign. We should not force them to support us. Let them go."

And so another two years passed. However, when King Wu and Jiang Shang learned that some significant incidents had taken place in the Shang court—some loyal high-ranking officials having been killed by the king—they knew it was finally time to attack Shang. Now nobody could save Shang and the king.

The army set off on the appointed day, when the main forces of the king of Shang were far away from the capital city, Chaoge. When King Wu and Jiang Shang entered the city, the nobility was terrified, while some of the Shang soldiers turned their weapons on their commanders.

The outcome was as expected. The king of Shang was forced to commit suicide and the Shang Dynasty came to its end. A new dynasty, the Zhou, was established. Jiang Shang, the prime minister who helped King Wen and King Wu found the new dynasty, became a lasting legend. As a symbol of wisdom, he became the hero of many tales. The book *Records of Spirits,* written by Gan Bao of the Eastern Jin Dynasty, includes many legends and detailed stories about Jiang Shang, King Wen and King Wu—many of which are still popular even today.

# Spring and Autumn Period
# (770-476 BC)

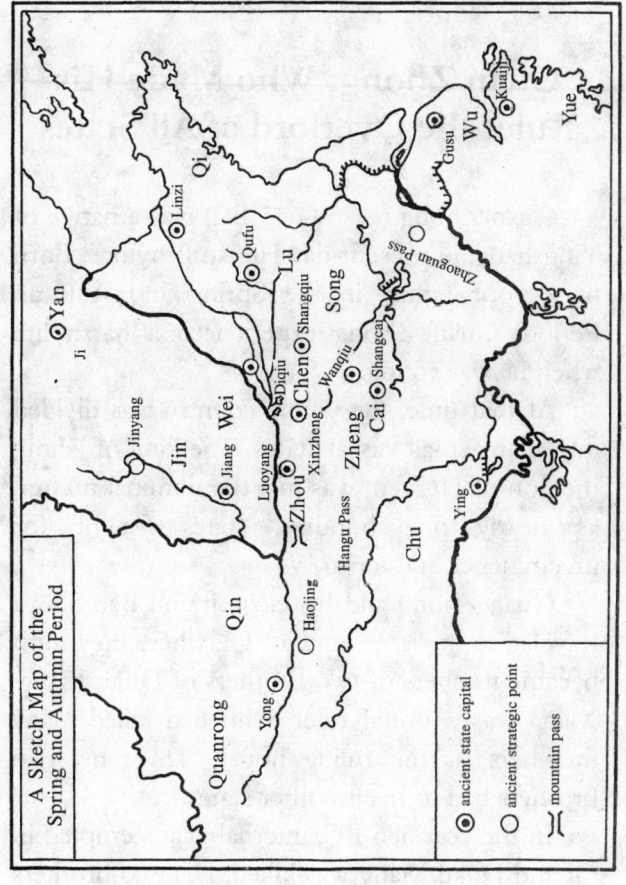

# Guan Zhong, Who Made His Ruler the Overlord of All States

Guan Zhong (*c*. 730-645 BC) was a native of Yingshang, in present-day Henan Province. Born to a poor family in the Spring and Autumn Period, Guan Zhong experienced a harsh life when he was young.

At that time, the whole country was divided into many small vassal states. The king of Zhou, the Son of Heaven, was just the nominal master, as nearly one hundred states fought for preeminence and territory.

Guan Zhong and his close friend Bao Shuya traveled to the large State of Qi, where they soon became teachers of two brothers of Duke Xiang. Xiang was a brutal ruler, who had killed many members of the ruling house. Thus, his two brothers had to flee to other states.

In the year 686 BC, internal chaos erupted in Qi and Duke Xiang was killed. His two brothers became rival successors to the throne of Qi. Guan Zhong and Bao Shuya each accompanied his own master to return to Qi to take the throne. It was clear that the quicker one would be crowned the new ruler.

Guan Zhong led several soldiers to stop his master's rival-brother, Xiao Bai, who was on his way to Qi. On encountering him, Guan Zhong shot an arrow at Xiao Bai. The arrow, however, did not pierce his body but struck the golden hook on his belt. Xiao Bai feigned death, then fled to the capital city of Qi.

Since Guan Zhong thought Xiao Bai dead, he returned to inform his own master. By the time they discovered Xiao Bai was still alive, it was too late.

Xiao Bai ascended the throne and became known as Duke Huan of Qi. The first thing he did was to eliminate his opponents, including his brother. His brother's followers such as Guan Zhong were also on his wanted list, and soon all were captured. When it came Guan Zhong's turn to be put to death, Bao Shuya stopped the duke: "Sire, if all you want is to administer Qi efficiently, I can do the job for you; but if you want to become the overlord of all states, Guan Zhong is the only man who can accomplish that."

The duke hesitated. After all, Guan Zhong

had once tried to kill him.

Bao Shuya insisted: "But he had reason then, since his master at that time was your rival. But now if you make him your prime minister, he will work loyally for you."

With the help of Bao Shuya, Guan Zhong finally found his place. Here, the great friendship between Bao Shuya and Guan Zhong deserves notice. They had been business partners before they came to Qi. Bao Shuya had not cared that Guan Zhong always took the lion's share. He always told others who had urged him to break his alliance with Guan Zhong: "Yiwu (another name for Guan Zhong) takes more because he is poor." Regretting his conduct, Guan Zhong always tried to make it up with his friend, but Bao Shuya had refused again and again.

In his earlier political career, Guan Zhong had experienced failure many times. While others thought Guan Zhong inept, Bao Shuya always stood up for him, arguing: "Yiwu is a man of talent, but he has never been given a proper chance. If he were to serve a wise ruler, everything would be different."

Guan Zhong is known to have always said: "My parents gave me life, but it is Bao Shuya who knows me better than anyone else. A friend in need is a friend indeed. Bao Shuya is just such a friend to me."

Although they had served different patrons when they both first took postings in Qi, they still held onto their friendship. This, certainly, would not have been easy for most people. Whenever Guan Zhong found himself in a precarious position, either in his life or in his political career, Bao Shuya always backed him.

On taking up his premiership, Guan Zhong launched a series of political, economic and military reforms. Guided by the principle that a state should be run to increase the wealth of the people, Guan Zhong focused on improving the overall strength of his state.

In terms of administration, Guan Zhong rearranged the old structures and set up a new system. Under this system, the state was divided at several levels, each level having to report to the level above it. This did much toward establishing social stability.

On military matters, Guan Zhong built up national guards similar to those in today's Switzerland. A military regimen was observed among the common people in the capital city, so if needed they could all be mobilized as soldiers in times of war. These soldiers-to-be were trained in their spare time. From those outside of the capital, Guan Zhong selected only the best as soldiers.

In terms of the economy, Guan Zhong encouraged individual economy and the privatization of land. He paid attention to agriculture as well as trade. With a reduction of taxes, commerce in Qi began to flourish.

A few years after implementing Guan Zhong's reforms, Qi became a powerful and wealthy state. Using diplomacy, Guan Zhong overcame some smaller states, while uniting with larger ones. Upholding a policy of supporting the Zhou ruler while defeating smaller tribes such as Shanrong and Yi, which had long brought trouble to the states like Yan, Cao, Song and Wei, Qi acquired a powerful reputation among all the states. Due to Qi's efforts, Shanrong and Yi were defeated and dared not interfere anymore with these states.

While Qi was aiding some states fight the Shanrong and Yi, the State of Chu, in southern China, saw an opportunity to expand north. Qi, by that time, had built itself into a position of preeminence among the states. On learning of Chu's plans, Qi soon organized the seven states of Lu, Song, Chen, Wei, Cao, Zheng and Xu and went into battle with Chu. Chu was certainly no match for Qi, and soon sued for peace. The subsequent treaty forced Chu to acknowledge

Qi's position as the overlord of all the states.

Soon after that, Guan Zhong encouraged Duke Huan to call many council meetings of rulers of all states across the kingdom. In the year 651 BC, when Qi called another council meeting in Kuiqiu, in present-day Henan Province, even the King of Zhou sent a delegate to take part. This signified that Duke Huan of Qi had reached the zenith of his career as an overlord.

Over a span of 30 years, Duke Huan realized his ambition of becoming the overlord of all the states. He was certainly a talented politician, but without Guan Zhong, his path to supremacy would have been much more protracted.

Guan Zhong was also a man of high integrity. After Qi defeated the State of Lu, Lu sued for peace and, as tribute, promised to give Qi a large swath of its territories. Duke Huan agreed and both parties signed a treaty at Ke, in present-day Shandong province. During the parley meeting, a soldier beside duke of Lu suddenly caught the duke of Qi with a sharp dagger, demanding he give back the Lu territory Qi had occupied. Under such duress, Duke Huan of Qi had to agree. Soon after, however, the duke felt quite vengeful and wanted to kill this soldier. Guan Zhong stopped him, saying: "Sire, you made a promise when you were caught by this soldier. No doubt you may be temporarily happy if you kill him and take back the territory—but you will also lose your credibility forever among all other states. Don't do such a thing!" Thus the duke of Qi returned the Lu territory. Upon hearing this, many states considered Qi a trustworthy state and sought alliances with it.

In the later years of his reign, it is said that Duke Huan of Qi only indulged in the pleasures of the senses. He dallied among a group of eunuchs and concubines all day and night. Besides advising the ruler, Guan Zhong was the one who had to devote himself totally to state affairs. But by the year 645 BC, Guan Zhong lay dying. The ruler visited Guan Zhong and asked him to name his successor to be the new prime minister. The records relate, in fact, that the ruler had three candidates in mind. The first was a man skillful at cuisine and flattery; the second, someone who had left his mother 15 years ago and refused to go back to visit her; the third was one who had made himself an eunuch in order to stay with the duke day and night. Certainly none of them would be suitable to be the prime minister of a big state. Guan Zhong replied in the negative regarding these three people and warned the duke to stay away from them. The duke ignored Guan Zhong's advice and appointed these three to key positions after Guan Zhong's death. As a result, when the duke was seriously ill, these three confined him to the palace. Duke Huan of Qi, at that time recalling what Guan Zhong had told him, is said to have sighed: "Guan Zhong was truly farsighted! I dare not face him in the nether world."

In Chinese history, Guan Zhong is remembered as a famous reformer. Accomplished at both politics and economic management, Guan Zhong with his foresight helped Duke Huan of Qi become overlord of all states in the early Spring and Autumn Period. He is also known for having promoted the development and reform of society, and many a statesman of later generations has held Guan Zhong up as a model prime minister, alongside that other famous prime minister in Chinese history: Zhuge Liang.

# Yan Ying, the Diminutive Yet Eloquent Prime Minister

Power flows from a person's mind, more than simply from his body. Believe it or not, Yan Ying is the perfect example of such a powerful wisdom.

Yan Ying (?-500 BC) was the prime minister to three successive rulers of the State of Qi during the Spring and Autumn Period. Known for his diplomatic genius, Yan Ying has been described as a most innovative and eloquent man. It is also known that Yan Ying was shorter than average height—though nobody dared look down on him.

The most famous tale of Yan Ying, which illustrates how powerful a small man can be, relates to the killing of three giants with two peaches. These three men had caused offense to Yan Ying. Though it was impossible for Yan Ying to fight even one of them, he still had his own way. He whispered to each giant: "The duke has granted two peaches to the other two men. It seems they are better than you." Hearing this, the three all became angry, as well as jealous of each other. Eventually, they decided to fight each other over honor. Unfortunately, they all died during the combat. Thus, Yan Ying, a diminutive man with little physical strength, using only two peaches, killed three men of a much greater strength.

Perhaps this tale gives the impression that Yan Ying was somewhat cruel as well as manipulative. More often though, Yan Ying put his wisdom and eloquence to good use in state affairs and diplomacy.

He once visited the State of Chu as Qi's envoy, at a time when Chu was stronger than Qi. The king of Chu, knowing Yan Ying to be a short man, intentionally opened a smaller gate beside the front gate so as to humiliate him. Yan Ying most assuredly refused to step through the small gate, and called out: "If I were to visit a dog's state, I would have to enter through a dog's gate. Since I'm in the State of Chu, I surely cannot enter through here." Hearing this, the Chu officials had to let Yan Ying through the main entrance.

When the king of Chu met Yan Ying, he asked: "So there is nobody else in your country?"

Yan Ying replied, "Most certainly not. We

have hundred of thousands of people."

The king continued, "Then why did they send *you* to my state?"

"According to our tradition, the most virtuous may visit the best country. I am the worst, so they let me visit Chu," Yan Ying calmly responded.

Several years later, Yan Ying visited Chu for the second time. Before his arrival, the king of Chu said to his followers: "Yan Ying is an articulate person. Any bright ideas for how to humiliate him this time?" One of his shrewdest officials suggested a ruse.

When Yan Ying arrived, the king welcomed him warmly and hosted a banquet in his honor. During the banquet, two soldiers escorted a man before the king. The king asked, "What wrong has he done?" One soldier replied, "This man of Qi has committed theft." The king turned to Yan Ying and said, "Is theft natural to the Qi people?" Yan Ying stood up and declared loudly: "I hear that oranges grow well south of the Yellow River, yet they always taste bad when grown north of the river. It depends on the water and the land. Qi people in the land of Qi seem well behaved; yet they commit theft when in Chu. Is something wrong with your water and your soil?" The king of Chu had nothing to say.

In state affairs, Yan Ying displayed even greater skill. Since the three dukes he served were not such virtuous rulers, Yan Ying always made use of proverbs and witticisms to influence these rulers to do what was best. In this way, his advice was more easily accepted.

Once when one of the duke's most treasured horses had died, he angrily ordered the horse's groom to be killed. Yan Ying stopped him and asked: "I wonder which of a man's parts Yao and Shun (virtuous rulers in ancient times) lopped off when they killed someone." The duke immediately realized that he had overreacted. He then ordered the groom jailed. Yan Ying insisted: "Sire, let me tell you what real crimes this groom has committed. First, as a groom, he let a horse die; second, the dead horse was the favorite of Your Highness; third, he made Your Highness kill a person because a horse was dead. People will hate Your Highness upon hearing this. If people hate Your Highness, other states will also look down upon Your Highness and the state." Hearing this, the ruler sighed: "Let him go, please. I don't want to ruin my name." Thus, with his wisdom, Yan Ying prevented an injustice.

Yan Ying took every opportunity to tell the

duke how a good ruler should act.

Once Duke Jing went to appreciate the scenery on Mount Niushan. Beholding the panoramic view of his beautiful capital city, he lamented: "How lovely my country is! Why must we all die and leave this homeland?"

On hearing this, two of his ministers said through their tears: "We have fared in this life much worse than Your Highness. Even so, we do not want to die. Why should you, Sire, even think of death?"

At this, Yan Ying chuckled. Puzzled, the duke asked Yan Ying: "Just now I was feeling very sad, and the other two ministers felt sad too. Why is it that you alone laughed?"

Yan Ying replied: "If virtuous dukes like Tai and Huan and brave dukes like Zhuang and Ling had not died but instead still retained their titles, Your Highness would now be a peasant working behind a plough. A ruler of a nation has a busy work schedule—is there any time for him to think of death? Your Highness can peacefully ascend the throne, because your predecessors have left this world one by one. Your crying for this, therefore, is against the principle of benevolence, and those who have cried together with you are mere sycophants. So I was merely laughing at an ungracious ruler and his obsequious ministers."

The duke felt ashamed, and made himself and the two officials each drink two cups of wine as punishment.

Yan Ying was most respected by the Qi people for his simple life. Even as prime minister, he ate and dressed like a common person. When the duke visited Yan Ying's home, he discovered Yan's wife to be old and ugly. On his own initiative, the ruler promised to grant some beautiful girls and land to Yan Ying.

Yan Ying refused and said, "I have no regrets about my poverty. Sire, if you wish to reward me, you can reduce people's taxes."

Located in the busy center of the city, Yan Ying's house was old and shabby. The duke then asked, "Why not move to a better place?"

Yan Ying replied, "I often wonder whether I am qualified to live here. To me it's a luxurious house. More importantly, it has helped me understand the lot of the common people. Really, it has aided me greatly in my dealing with state affairs."

The duke smiled, saying, "Well, since you live in the center of the city, do you know what is of value and what is cheap?"

"Certainly," Yan Ying replied.

"Tell me," the ruler urged.

"Many Qi people are often punished by having their feet cut off, so artificial limbs are expensive while straw sandals are cheap."

On hearing this, the duke was so shocked he then ordered the commutation of such punishments.

As a prime minister, Yan Ying demonstrated remarkable genius. With extraordinary wisdom and eloquence, Yan Ying played a vital role in maintaining the stability of Qi. In *Records of the Historian*, Sima Qian admired Yan Ying so much he said he would have wished to carry Yan Ying's riding whip and follow him.

# Wu Zixu, Whose Hair Turned White Overnight

One of the most famous Peking Opera routines, *Wenzhao Pass*, is based on an episode about Prime Minister Wu Zixu who lived during the Spring and Autumn Period. As the opera recounts, while fleeing to the State of Wu to seek asylum, Wu Zixu found his way blocked at Wenzhao Pass. Unable to break through, with his enemies hot on his trail, Wu Zixu found himself at his wits' end. It is recorded that so great was the peril, Wu Zixu's hair turned white overnight. Since Wu Zixu lived more than 2,000 years ago, no one knows if this particular tale is, in fact, true or not. However, the opera is based on a real person, and here is his story.

Wu Yuan (?-484 BC), whose given name was Zixu, was a native of the State of Chu during the Spring and Autumn Period. He was born into an aristocratic family and both his father and grandfather were high-ranking officials, famous for speaking frankly and directly with their kings. Wu Zixu inherited this trait and earned the respect

of many through his solid character and his willingness to accept criticism.

One of his father's political opponents was a devious and fawning official called Fei Wuji. Fei made false accusations against the elder Wu which unfortunately the king believed, ordering the honest official's execution. Fei then feared that the innocent man's sons would avenge their father's death and thus plotted to kill them all. Only Wu Zixu was able to escape death and was forced to flee into exile.

One day, he climbed the summit of one of the peaks in the Taihang Mountains and sighed as he gazed on the lands of the State of Zheng.

"Zheng is strategically located and its people are considerate, but the ruler is said to be heartless. I will not offer my services to him."

He then traveled to the State of Xu. There he gained an audience with the ruler, but Xu was weak and feared the wrath of Chu if he were to harbor the fugitive. Once more, Wu Zixu had to set off on his travels.

On his way to seek asylum in the State of Wu, he came to Wenzhao Pass. Troops stationed there had received orders to arrest him as the army of Chu were closing in on him. A huge reward had been offered for his capture and his way was fraught with danger. He found his way to the mighty Yangtze River, where an old boatman saved his life by ferrying him across to the other side. In gratitude, Wu Zixu offered him his precious sword as a reward, but when the old man refused to accept it, Wu Zixu was deeply moved.

Wu Zixu pressed onward in his flight, exposed to the cold and rain. Since he had no money to pay for food, he had to beg the whole way. Finally, he arrived in the State of Wu, but not knowing what the Wu king's attitude would be toward him, he did not venture to seek an audience straight away. Instead, Wu Zixu played the flute, begging for food in the streets.

One day, Ji Guang, the king's cousin, came upon Wu Zixu and, on learning more about this mysterious beggar, recommended him to the king. Thus, Wu Zixu's fortunes began to change.

The king was very kind to Wu Zixu and appreciated his political acumen. For his part, Wu Zixu considered this an opportunity to use the power of the State of Wu to seek revenge on the State of Chu. And so a close relationship developed between the two men. As time went on, however, Wu Zixu came to realize that the king was not an adept politician. Ji Guang, on the other hand, seemed to be a very ambitious man with greater judgement, talent and courage. Wu

Zixu decided to retire temporarily from political life and bide his time.

As a possible successor to the throne, Ji Guang had long planned to seize power. His opportunity arrived, and in 515 BC Ji Guang killed the king during a banquet and pronounced himself King of Wu. He took the title King He Lü of Wu, and appointed Wu Zixu as his senior minister.

With the help of Wu Zixu, the State of Wu became more and more powerful by the day.

In the year 512 BC, the State of Wu launched its first attack on the State of Chu. The war lasted six years, and the State of Chu's vitality was drained. In the year 506 BC, together with two other states, the State of Wu launched a massive attack on Chu. They easily occupied its capital, Ying, but the king of Chu managed to escape.

The old king of Chu, who had put Wu Zixu's father and elder brother to death, had already died. Wu Zixu now opened the tomb of the dead king and whipped his corpse three hundred times. His actions stirred the wrath of a Chu official, who vowed to save his state and sought the help of the State of Qin. In the face of this alliance, Wu was forced to withdraw from Chu.

While Wu and Chu had been waging war, the

neighboring State of Yue had grown yet more and more powerful.

In the year 496 BC, a new king, Gou Jian, ascended the throne of the State of Yue. King He Lü decided that this was an opportunity to strike a blow at the newly thriving State of Yue. His plans were thwarted, however, when Yue ambushed his troops. The Wu army was badly defeated and King He Lü fatally wounded. After the death of He Lü, his son, Fu Chai, took the throne and swore to wipe out the State of Yue. Wu Zixu had by now become prime minister of the State of Wu.

In the year 494 BC, the Wu army inflicted a terrible defeat on the army of Yue. King Gou Jian was forced to retreat to Guiji Mountain. Yue's senior minister, Wen Zhong, now bribed Bo Pi, a high-ranking official of Wu, and through him sued for peace. At the same time, he promised to send some beautiful women from Yue as a gift to King Fu Chai. Among these was Xi Shi, famous for being one of the four most beautiful women in the history of China. She was so beautiful, it is said, that the moon hid its face and flowers blushed in shame at the sight of her.

After Bo Pi had been bought off, he convinced King Fu Chai to accept Yue's offer.

Wu Zixu tried hard to persuade the king not to do so, saying: "Gou Jian can swallow humiliation and bear the heaviest of burdens. If we do not kill him today, future trouble is certain." Yet Fu Chai ignored his advice. Wu Zixu sighed, "A sea of troubles awaits the State of Wu."

Gou Jian, now a captive, served as Fu Chai's slave for three years. He demeaned himself before Fu Chai, but at the same time continued to bribe Bo Pi. With the help of Bo Pi, Gou Jian won the trust of Fu Chai, who eventually decided to release his captive. Again, Wu Zixu warned the king, "If we do not kill the king of Yue today, he will certainly take revenge in the future." But, again, his words went unheeded.

Gou Jian soon returned to the State of Yue. He now "slept on brushwood and tasted gall," to remind himself of his shame so as to nurture his desire for vengeance. He set to work training his troops and having weapons made, preparing for the day when he would destroy his enemy. At the same time, through bribery and intrigue, he lulled Fu Chai into a false sense of security, while sowing discord between the king and his officials.

According to some legends, Xi Shi was a beautiful spy sent by Gou Jian. Fu Chai was so enamored that he had a special palace built for her, and acceded to all her wishes. Xi Shi soon discovered that, unlike other officials, Wu Zixu was steadfast and true to the State of Wu. She lost no opportunity to speak ill of the prime minister to the king, as did Wu Zixu's political opponent, the crafty official Bo Pi. King Fu Chai came to dislike his prime minister more and more.

In the year 484 BC, Fu Chai was planning to attack the State of Qi. Wu Zixu disagreed, saying: "Your Majesty, the customs and speech of Qi are very different to those of Wu. Even if we were to succeed in subduing Qi, we would have great difficulty in ruling and absorbing its people. The State of Yue, on the other hand, shares with us both customs and language. This means that Yue itself could conquer and swallow us as easily as we could them. We should launch a preemptive strike against Yue before turning attention to our old rival Qi."

Bo Pi objected: "Your Majesty would be unwise to heed this advice. Yue is insignificant in this struggle for supremacy among great powers. The subjugation of Yue would do little to enhance your might and prestige among states. A swift conquest of Qi would force the capitulation of Jin and project the supremacy of your realm across the Central Plain."

King Fu Chai, persuaded by Bo Pi's words, ordered a general mobilization for a campaign against Qi.

Wu Zixu now enraged his king by saying, "I venture to predict, Sire, that victory over Qi will result in the annihilation of our state."

Fu Chai did in fact defeat Qi, and upon his return, ordered Wu Zixu executed. After the death sentence pronounced, Wu Zixu responded, "I beg you, Your Majesty, to at least preserve one of my eyes, so it may one day see the inevitable destruction of the State of Wu by Yue." With this, he cut his own throat and died on the spot. Fu Chai, in contempt, had both of Wu Zixu's eyes gouged out and his dead body hung on the capital's eastern gate which faced the State of Yue.

"Now, you will be able to see the Yue army advancing on Wu—if they ever come!" he told the dead man.

Just over a decade later, the fortunes of Yue revived, and it once more became a powerful state. It occupied the capital of Wu, destroyed Fu Chai's ancestral temple, and captured Fu Chai alive. Before killing himself, Fu Chai regretted that he had not listened to Wu Zixu, lamenting: "If the shadows of the netherworld know everything that goes on here on earth, how will I face Zixu when we meet?"

# Fan Li, Prime Minister to a Titan

There is a beautiful grove called Li's Garden in Wuxi City, Jiangsu Province. It is named after Fan Li, the prime minister of the State of Yue in the Spring and Autumn Period, who lived there after he resigned from political office. An even more romantic anecdote claims Fan Li lived in this garden with Xi Shi, one of the four most beautiful women in Chinese history.

According to some versions of the legend, Fan Li and Xi Shi were lovers. In order to save both the State of Yue and Gou Jian, the king of Yue who had been held in captivity in the State of Wu, Xi Shi decided to sacrifice herself. It was a painful decision for both Fan Li and Xi Shi. In the end, for the sake of the kingdom, Xi Shi became King Fu Chai of Wu's concubine and played a key role in Yue defeating Wu.

Having saved Yue from Wu's designs, Fan Li believed he had reached the apex of his career as Yue's prime minister, and felt it time to resign. Xi Shi, meanwhile, had fled from the State of Wu. Leaving behind a perilous political life, Fan Li finally reunited with his sweetheart and brought her to what became known as Li's Garden. And Fan Li, being quite shrewd, soon became a successful merchant. The tale, of course, always ends with the enterprising Fan Li and the beautiful Xi Shi living a blissful, affluent life together.

But let us now try to uncover the true story of Fan Li.

Born into a poor family in the State of Chu, Fan Li was quite ambitious when he was young. Not having even one close friend made him forlorn and unruly, causing neighbors to think he was crazy. Fortunately, a local official named Wen Zhong saw something more in him, and visited him so often that they finally became fast friends.

Both of them wanted to leave the State of Chu, and looked everywhere for an opportunity to use their talents to the full.

When they arrived at the State of Yue, Gou Jian, the ruler of Yue, warmly welcomed them and offered them high-ranking positions.

At that time, Yue and Wu were as hostile as fire and water. Gou Jian had defeated the Wu army, and the ruler of Wu, He Lü, had just died from his serious injuries. Fu Chai, the new king of Wu, had sworn to take vengeance, and Gou

Jian decided he must strike first. Fan Li resolutely disagreed, pointing out that the moment was not right at all for a war against the State of Wu. The stubborn-headed Gou Jian ignored Fan Li's advice and launched an attack on Wu in the year 494 BC.

Unfortunately, it turned out that Fan Li's advice was absolutely correct. Gou Jian and his Yue army were soundly defeated by the Wu army, bringing the State of Yue to the brink of destruction.

Gou Jian now turned to Fan Li for guidance on what to do next. Fan Li gave him three suggestions: first, Gou Jian and his wife should beg Fu Chai for mercy by presenting him with invaluable gifts including beautiful women and treasures; second, they should submit to becoming Fu Chai's slaves; third, they should bribe a high-ranking official in Wu, Bo Pi. This time around, Gou Jian followed Fan Li's instructions, and the State of Yue escaped annihilation.

Leaving his own kingdom, Gou Jian appointed Fan Li to manage Yue's state affairs. Fan Li instead recommended Wen Zhong for the job, and volunteered to join Gou Jian in his harsh life as slave to the State of Wu.

Although they were all slaves in Wu, Fan Li

still regarded Gou Jian as his master. In the master's presence, Fan Li always showed great respect toward Gou Jian.

One day when Fu Chai met Fan Li, he said: "Gifted people should never serve a state in decline. Why not ally yourself with Wu instead of remaining a slave?"

Fan Li replied, "I have no other ambition but to follow my master."

Fu Chai then threatened Fan Li, "If you resist, I shall imprison you."

Fan Li only replied, "Yes, Your Majesty." Thus, at a loss how to persuade Fan Li, the rival king had to give up.

During Gou Jian's three-year sojourn in the State of Wu, Fu Chai was impressed by the old king's behavior. When Fu Chai fell ill once, and did not recover for a long time, Fan Li found his opportunity: he spread a rumor that only human flesh could heal Fu Chai, then convinced Gou Jian to cut a piece of flesh from his leg and offer it to Fu Chai. Fu Chai was deeply moved and soon recovered. After this incident, Fu Chai decided to free Gou Jian and Fan Li. Although his prime minister Wu Zixu tried to restrain him, he still persisted in his folly.

Gou Jian was enormously grateful for Fan Li's loyalty and wisdom. He told Fan Li, "From now on, my kingdom is yours!" After that, Fan Li became prime minister of the State of Yue, as well as its most respected official.

In order not to forget his enslavement and shame in the State of Wu, Gou Jian, as it is said, "slept on brushwood and tasted gall" every day.

Eager for revenge, the king constantly wanted to attack Wu, but Fan Li would restrain him. Fan Li reminded him: "Wu is still stronger than Yue. We are not ready for vengeance. Sire, you must be patient and conceal your intentions, instead of acting rashly and blindly. At present, you should concentrate only on strengthening Yue."

With Fan Li and Wen Zhong's help, Gou Jian implemented a series of policies to develop the economy and rebuild the army. It took the State of Yue ten years to recover from its near annihilation.

At the same time, using Fan Li and Wen Zhong's schemes, Yue built up friendly relations with such powerful states as Chu and Jin on the one hand, and on the other, lulled Wu while secretly gauging its flaws.

Fan Li himself presented the tribute of treasures and women to Fu Chai. Among the women, Xi Shi was the most beautiful. She quickly won the favor of Fu Chai, who built a special palace where he could dally with Xi Shi night and day.

This was only the beginning of the plot. In order to obtain grain from Wu, Gou Jian falsely claimed that Yue had suffered a disaster. In this way, Yue augmented its own supplies while consuming Wu's grain.

Making use of Fu Chai's ambition to become supreme ruler of all states across the land, Fan Li told Fu Chai that Yue would assist Wu if Wu would launch a northern expedition.

Fu Chai's suspicions about Yue were thus lulled. His next most fatal mistake was to kill his loyal prime minister Wu Zixu, an injustice Gou Jian and Fan Li observed with great satisfaction.

When Fu Chai launched his war for supremacy far away from his own state, Fan Li told Gou Jian, "Sire, now is the time for us to take revenge."

Since most of Wu's troops were fighting in the north, those remaining were only the old and weak. Yue troops soon entered Wu's capital city, Gusu (present-day Suzhou), and killed the crown prince. Fu Chai heard the news and rushed back. He sent an envoy to sue for peace. Fan Li said to Gou Jian, "Sire, although we have delivered a massive blow to Wu, we are not yet strong enough to eliminate it. Accept Fu Chai's offer."

Several years later, the Yue troops again defeated Wu. Fu Chai again sent an envoy to Yue. This time, Fu Chai asked Gou Jian not to destroy Wu given his earlier benevolence when Yue had been defeated many years before. Gou Jian and Wen Zhong wanted to absolve Fu Chai, but Fan Li firmly disagreed. He said, "Sire, have you forgotten your humiliation? What were you waiting for all these years? When Heaven presented Yue to Wu, Fu Chai did not accept. That is his fault. Today, when Heaven presents Wu to Yue, we should not disobey the will of the gods."

When Fu Chai heard Yue's refusal for peace, he committed suicide with his own sword.

Yue, having finally eliminated Wu, grew more powerful than ever before.

Gou Jian, clearly grateful for Fan Li's key role in defeating Wu, appointed him commander-in-chief of Yue troops. Fan Li thus became the most powerful and respected official in the State of Yue.

But as Chinese saying goes, "To consort with a king is tantamount to living with a tiger." Fan Li realized that it was especially dangerous to keep company with a king as triumphant as Gou

Jian. He felt he should resign while the going was good. He told this to his close friend Wen Zhong, wishing for them to leave Gou Jian together. But Wen Zhong refused. Fan Li then said, "I am most anxious about your future. Have you ever heard the saying, 'once all the hares are bagged, the hunting dogs are killed for food.' So will we be. When we have outlived our usefulness, we will be eliminated." Wen Zhong considered his words to be overly melodramatic and insisted on staying put. Fan Li is said to have bid farewell to his friend with a sigh.

Once he had traveled beyond Taihu Lake, Fan Li sent a messenger to inform Gou Jian of his resignation. Nobody knew where Fan Li had gone. Gou Jian felt sick at heart on hearing the news. He let people sculpt a bronze statue of Fan Li beside his throne. Every morning Gou Jian would salute Fan Li's statue. Moreover, he granted Fan's family a large estate in honor of Fan Li's great achievements.

Fan Li changed his name and migrated to the State of Qi (today's Shandong Province). Qi was a state with flourishing commerce. Fan Li was so clever that he soon became a successful merchant.

When the ruler of Qi discovered Fan Li's

good name, he asked Fan Li to be his prime minister. Fan Li, having no interest at all in politics anymore, had to leave the state surreptitiously.

This time he came to a central location named Tao (now Dingtao, Shandong Province). He called himself Master Taozhu, and soon rebuilt his merchant empire in this new locale. It is said that the extent of his properties was as vast as a state.

But Fan Li was no common merchant—he had once been a prime minister. After he had accumulated great wealth through all his wheeling and dealing, Fan Li felt he had finally achieved his goal. He did not care how much he had saved, but instead often donated his money and riches to the poor—for he knew that he could, whenever needed, earn as much money as he wanted.

Fan Li's repute as a merchant of great wealth extended far beyond his time. Later merchants and traders worshipped him as their antecedent and model. In China, "trade" also has another name: "Taozhu industry." Many books about trade have liked to use Fan Li's name, since it represents authority.

What about Xi Shi? According to some historical records, Gou Jian threw Xi Shi into a river after Wu was eliminated. Despite her sacrifice, this beautiful lady has often been depicted as a temptress, bringing on grief and disaster.

As for Wen Zhong, just as Fan Li sadly predicted, he was killed arbitrarily by Gou Jian. Wen Zhong is said to have cried before his death: "Oh, what a terrible mistake I made! I should have listened to Fan Li…."

# Shang Yang, the Great Reformer

Shang Yang (390-338 BC) was originally known as Gongsun Yang. His ancestors had been rulers of Wei in the Spring and Autumn Period, but his family was in decline by the time of the Warring States Period.

As a young man, Shang Yang had worked under Gongsun Cuo, the prime minister of the State of Wei. When Gongsun Cuo fell seriously ill, the king of Wei visited him, and asked: "Who shall be your successor?"

Gongsun Cuo replied, "Gongsun Yang is a man of great ability. However, if you decide not to use him, then you should kill him for the sake of our state." The king said nothing and left.

Gongsun Cuo then spoke to Shang Yang and requested he leave at once. He decided to tell this to Shang Yang after regretting what he had said to the king. He added: "It seems the king will not accept my proposal. You had better leave here as quickly as possible, or you will be trapped."

Shang Yang replied: "If the king ignores your advice to use me, why would he kill me as you have advised?" And so he stayed put in Wei.

The king meanwhile returned to his palace and said to his men, "You see, Gongsun Cuo must be really sick, recommending Gongsun Yang as his successor. He's losing his mind!"

Sometime later Gongsun Cuo died, and Shang Yang, having no other reason to stay in Wei, upon hearing of Qin's call for people of talent, went to Qin.

Introduced by a Qin official, Shang Yang met duke Xiao of Qin at his palace. At first, Shang Yang talked of the duties of rulers, but the duke showed little interest and fell asleep. Then, Shang Yang changed topics and described how to make the state powerful and prosperous. Apparently, the duke enjoyed this topic very much for they talked tirelessly for several days.

Duke Xiao finally agreed with Shang Yang about the need for reform, but he was afraid of being criticized by other officials and his people, so he called for a court discussion.

Shang Yang aired his opinions first: "Those who hesitate achieve nothing. It is not unusual that those who have great ability are blamed by the worldly; that those who have unique ideas are slandered by ordinary people. The stupid never understand things happening in front of them, while the intelligent may know things ahead of time. As for ordinary people, you need not discuss matters with them, they will follow anything readymade. So, a ruler need not follow old regulations and laws if he strengthens the state; he need not abide by tradition if his people benefit from what he has done."

The duke concurred.

Another official, Gan Long, said: "I disagree. He who goes with tradition easily gains the support of officials and ordinary people."

Shang Yang replied: "Gan Long's talk is vulgar. The great dynasties before us implemented different laws and regulations. I wonder which tradition we should follow, do you mind answering me, Your Excellency Gan Long?"

Then Du Ji, another official, responded: "Sir, change is not worthwhile if we cannot reap a hundred-fold profit. Yet we will never falter if we follow ancient laws."

"Great rulers such as King Tang of Shang and King Wu of Zhou did not follow the ancients, yet they succeeded; while brutal kings such as Jie and Zhou followed the ancients and came to a tragic end. Those who are against ancient laws should not be chastised; those who follow ancient laws should not be praised." In this way, Shang Yang won a clear victory at this court debate, and the duke then ordered the reforms implemented.

Before the proclamation of the new laws, Shang Yang knew they would have to win the people's confidence. He ordered a stone column erected by the south gate of the market. He then announced: "Whoever can lift this column and carry it to the north gate will be offered a reward of ten gold pieces."

At first, people felt this to be rather strange and nobody dared try, not trusting Shang Yang's word. Then, Shang Yang added: "Whoever can lift this column and carry it to the north gate will be offered a reward of fifty gold pieces."

Finally one man plucked up the courage and lifted the column and carried it to the north gate. He was immediately offered a reward of fifty gold pieces. In such unusual ways, Shang Yang won the confidence of the people. The duke then formally proclaimed the new laws.

During the first year of implementing the new laws, thousands of people came to the capital city to complain about them. Even the crown prince had violated the new laws.

Shang Yang pointed out: "If those at the top are the first to break the law, for sure the law will not work." Then Shang Yang asked that the prince be penalized. However, since the prince was the heir to the throne and could not be punished, his mentors were punished instead. The new laws worked effectively after that.

Ten years after promulgating the new laws, Qin became wealthy and prosperous. Ordinary people were also very satisfied with the new laws. Those who had gone to the capital to complain about the new laws now returned singing the praises of the same laws.

After Qin became powerful and wealthy, visitors from many other states congratulated Duke Xiao. Shang Yang said to the duke: "Wei is our neighbor. Because of Wei's geographical position, they may attack Qin when the time is right. Qin has become stronger than ever before due to your wise rule, while Wei has just been defeated by Qi. The time is right to attack Wei and occupy strategic locations, which will help you become overlord of all states." The duke approved of Shang Yang's plan to attack Wei and appointed him Commander-in-chief.

Before the battle, Shang Yang wrote to Wei's general, Gongzi Ying. His letter read: "We were good friends when I worked in Wei. Although we are now generals of two opposing sides, I really do not want war with you. Why not have a drink together and sign an agreement? Then both of us can withdraw and maintain the safety of our two states."

Gongzi Ying took Shang Yang at his word, and met him for a drink. Suddenly, many soldiers rushed out and arrested Gongzi Ying. Shang Yang then launched an attack on Wei. Without a general, the Wei troops were soon defeated. The ruler of Wei had to sue for peace, and key territories were handed over to Qin. The king of Wei, the same king who had let Shang Yang leave without killing him, expressed his regret: "I should have listened to Gongsong Cuo's advice."

During his ten-year political career as Qin's prime minister, many aristocrats and officials came to deeply despise Shang Yang. Once a prince named Min broke the new laws and was punished, causing hatred against Shang Yang to breed in the minds of his followers.

One day, a man named Zhao Liang was introduced to Shang Yang. He told Shang Yang: "Sir, you have been extending your authority and silencing your critics in an unusual way. The strict implementation of the laws, and even penalizing the nobility, let alone members of the royal family, has alienated many people. I don't think you will live to a ripe old age if you keep acting this way. The best thing you can do now is to resign while there is no crisis. Your position is dangerous like the time just before dawn when the dew drops will vapor in the morning. If the duke dies, you will not last. I do not need to tell you how many people want you arrested and even killed."

Shang Yang, however, disregarded Zhao Liang's warning.

Five months later, Duke Xiao of Qin died and the crown prince took the throne. His followers then accused Shang Yang of treason. The new ruler had certainly also not forgotten what Shang Yang had once done to him. He ordered the arrest of Shang Yang.

Shang Yang fled to the border and tried to stay at an inn. The innkeeper, not recognizing him, said: "According to Shang Yang's new laws, we cannot take in guests without an identity card, for which both of us will be punished." Shang Yang sighed, "Oh, what an irony!"

Then he left Qin for Wei, but the people there hated him for his deceiving of Gongzi Ying and the defeating of the Wei army. They refused his request for asylum. Shang Yang then had to plan to flee to another state. However, certain Wei people had resolved: "We shall not let Shang Yang go. He is a criminal who has escaped Qin, a powerful state. To protect ourselves, we should deliver Shang Yang to Qin."

And so Shang Yang was sent back to Qin. As soon as Shang Yang entered Qin territory, he withdrew into his own fief and called on local troops to resist. The battle, however, ended quickly. Shang Yang was killed by Duke Hui of Qin, and his corpse was torn asunder by five chariots. His family was also eliminated.

Thus, Shang Yang died, but his new laws remained in force in the State of Qin, helping it become the most powerful state in the Warring States Period. It is as a reformer that Shang Yang truly succeeded. Therefore Shang Yang is still remembered as a great radical reformer to this day.

# Warring States Period
# (475-221 BC)

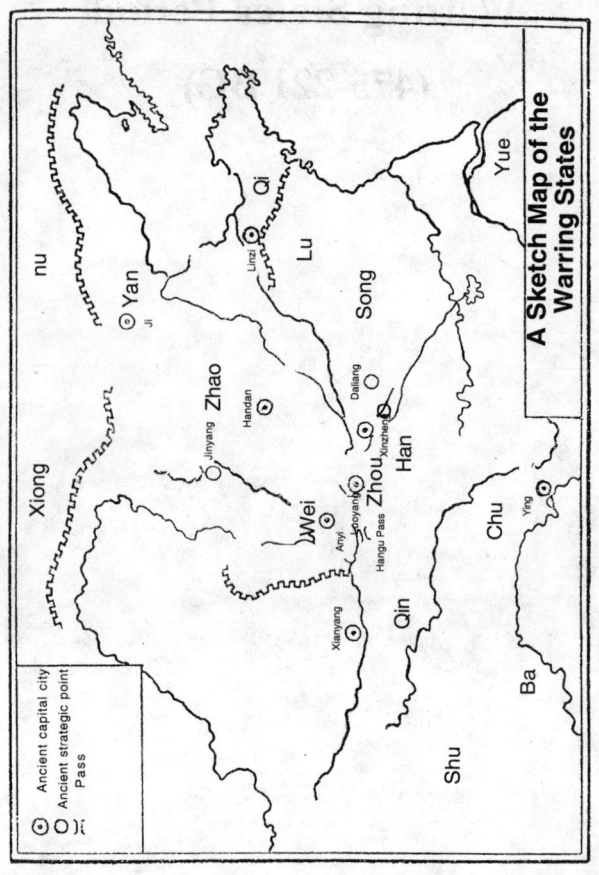

# Su Qin, Prime Minister of Six States

In the final years of the Warring States Period, Qin was the most powerful state among seven states of the country. As Qin grew more dominant day by day, its ambition to unite China grew more apparent. Alliances, among two, three or more states, were very much the order of the day. This need heralded the advent of a new popular profession: the Zonghenjia, or a political strategist whose main job was to sound out the rulers of different states so as to secure allies when required. Su Qin (?-284 BC), a legendary prime minister in Chinese history, was the most outstanding political strategist and ambassador of the time.

Born to a peasant family in the suburbs of Luoyang (in present-day Henan Province), Su Qin liked to study not farming or commerce, but political strategy. Su Qin, together with his two brothers, thus mastered this science.

It is recorded that Su Qin once studied under a famous recluse, Guiguzi, on Mount Yangcheng (in present-day Henan). After completing his studies, he traveled among several states, but was always snubbed. When he went back home, his family members also spurned him. They all thought Su Qin was indulging in what could not be seen as a genuine career in the traditional sense. To Su Qin's mind, however, his ambitions were of great import.

To arm himself with profound understanding, Su Qin studied extremely hard. He tied his hair to the beam of his house and pricked himself with a needle to keep awake when he felt sleepy late at night. This anecdote is still popular in China and gave rise to a well-known idiom to that effect. In this way, Su Qin studied for one year, developing his own analysis and strategies to deal with the current situation.

He set out on his travels once more. He arrived at the State of Yan in the midst of calamitous events. The King of Yan, he discovered, had ignored state affairs and let his prime minister rule, resulting in a palace coup. Grabbing the opportunity, Qi had attacked Yan and soon occupied many of its cities. The newly chosen king was also killed by Qi troops, and it was under such circumstances that King Zhao of Yan ascended the throne, vowing to avenge this humiliation. The King pronounced that Yan would welcome people of various talents, and thus, Su Qin, the famous general Yue Yi and many other eminent statesmen came to serve at the court of Yan.

Su Qin told the King: "Sire, if you want to overwhelm the more powerful Qi, you have to destroy it from the inside. I would like to be your spy in Qi."

The King appointed Su Qin his prime minister and sent him to work in Qi. Before leaving Yan, Su Qin told the King a story:

A long long time ago, an official had to leave his wife for a while to take up a post far away from his home. His wife had an affair with another man, though her paramour always worried about the day the official would come back. The wife then prepared a cup of poisoned wine to give her husband when he returned. When the official came home, the wife ordered a maid to pour the wine for him. The maid knew the wine was poisoned, and was in a dilemma: if she presented the wine, she would be the murderer; if she told the truth, her mistress would be divorced by her husband. In order to preserve their relationship, the maid dropped the cup onto the ground. The official, not knowing the truth, punished the maid by whipping her.

Through his parable, Su Qin wanted to tell

the King that faithful servants are sometimes punished for their loyalty. He said, "Sire, you shouldn't let other officials ruin our plans."

On meeting King Xuan of Qi, Su Qin congratulated him at first and then broke into a lament. The ruler was perplexed and asked for an explanation.

Su Qin replied: "I've heard that even a starving person will not eat poison. The King of Yan is the son-in-law of the King of Qin. Sire, you have occupied many cities belonging to Yan, which means you have set yourself against the powerful Qin. What difference is there between your deed and the eating of poison?"

On hearing this, the ruler of Qi urged Su Qin to tell him what to do. Su Qin then told him to return Yan's cities. The King was most happy to do that, and thus Su Qin's first goal was achieved.

In the year 300 BC, King Xuan of Qi died and King Min ascended the throne. Lord Mengchang, who was appointed his prime minister, was known for his hospitality, and Su Qin was always his frequent guest.

The King of Qin, long aware of Mengchang's eminence, invited Mengchang to be the prime minister of Qin. Lord Mengchang was most pleased to offer his services to the State of Qin.

His aides all tried to prevent him from going, but to no avail. "I have heard all your arguments before," he said, "but I am not convinced. If any one of you has anything new to tell me, let him speak up. Otherwise, remain silent."

Su Qin stepped forward and, upon being bidden to speak, said, "On my way here today, I passed the Zishui River. There I saw two figures shimmering above the water. One was made of clay, and the other of wood. I heard the latter say to the former: 'You are made of clay, any shower of rain will turn you into a mere dollop of mud.' The clay image replied, 'That's true, if I meet rain I will return to nature. But what about you? You are made from the wood of a peach tree in the Eastern Garden. A shower of rain would have you floating off down the river to heaven-knows-where.' Now, my Lord, you want to offer your services to the State of Qin, which has cast a greedy eye on the Central Plain. If you go, you will, like those figures, be completely at the mercy of fate."

Lord Mengchang pondered this awhile in the audience hall, and then left without a word. From then on, he never again spoke of going to the State of Qin.

In the year 296 BC, the peaceful relations between Yan and Qi broke down. As the ambassador of Yan, Su Qin had to return to Yan.

Two years later, the State of Qin asked Yan to persuade Qi to attack Song. Considering the plan opportune for Yan, King Zhao of Yan again sent Su Qin to Qi.

This time, Su Qin received a warm welcome from the ruler of Qi. Su Qin, the most outstanding ambassador of his time, succeeded again. King Min of Qi attacked Song and advanced to victory. This strengthened the ruler's trust of Su Qin. Later, he even appointed Su Qin prime minister. Su Qin's being a spy sent by Yan, his becoming prime minister of Qi was ironic. This proved how successful a role Su Qin had played, as a spy and an ambassador.

When relations between Qin and Qi began to worsen, the ruler of Qi resolved to unite with the other five states to attack Qin. Then, as an ambassador of Qi, Su Qin traveled among the five states.

Although Qin was the common enemy of these six states, they each had different interests. At first, the Qi ruler did not believe Yan, and so Su Qin requested the King of Yan to dispatch troops to support the six-state alliance. After that, he went to the southern states of Zhao and Wei. This time he had a double assignment: on the surface, he was an envoy of Qi, sent to organize the six-state alliance; in fact, he was a spy for Yan, sent to persuade Zhao and Wei to fight alongside Qi.

In the year 287 BC, a six-state alliance was set up. As its organizer, Su Qin is said to have possessed the prime ministerial seals of these six states, by which time, Su Qin had reached the peak of his political career.

When he went back home, family members who had been cold to him before, now showed great respect for him. He asked them, "Last time I came home, you were arrogant to me, why are you extremely deferential this time?" His relatives replied, "Because today you are different. You have a high-ranking position and countless wealth." Su Qin could not help but sigh, "A man who is rich is feared by his relatives; a man who is poor, looked down on. If his closest relatives act this way, why speak of others."

Although the six-state alliance was successfully forged, they were each just waiting for the others to act, thus, no state was really prepared to launch an attack on the State of Qin.

King Zhao of Yan, believing Su Qin had won the trust of the ruler of Qi, felt it was time for Yan to take revenge. Su Qin advised that Yan should await the best time. This aroused the suspicions of the King of Yan, despite the fact that Su Qin remained loyal to Yan and he was still working on persuading the State of Zhao to fight with Qi.

King Zhao of Yan grew more and more disillusioned with Su Qin's plan, and even recalled Su Qin back to Yan. Su Qin wrote a letter in response to him asking him to be patient. King Zhao ignored his plea and together with other states launched an attack on Qi.

Su Qin's cover as a spy for Yan was now laid bare. The enraged King of Qi sentenced Su Qin to death. Su Qin was torn asunder by five charitos -- one of the cruelest punishments in ancient China.

As Yan's spy, Su Qin had also managed to become the prime minister of Qi and possess the official seals of six states. He had successfully won the trust of the ruler of Qi and organized a six-state alliance to fight the powerful Qin— before he lost everything when his impatient king acted against his advice. The anecdote of his methods of studying hard is still popular in today's China.

# Lord Mengchang the Hospitable

During the Warring States Period, there were four nobles known for treating people of ability well. Tian Wen, popularly known as Lord Mengchang of the State of Qi is among these four patricians.

Born to the Qi royal family, Tian Wen's father, Tian Ying, was King Xuan's brother. Having more than forty sons, Tian Ying almost abandoned Tian Wen when he was born, simply because he did not like Tian Wen's birthday. His mother, however, secretly brought Tian Wen up, and it was only as an adult that Tian Wen met his father for the first time.

Because of his early setback, Tian Wen resolved to change his father's view of him. He argued ardently with his father on several occasions. And as a result, Tian Ying experienced a change of heart about his spurned son and selected Tian Wen as his successor.

After Tian Wen became his own master, he was a popular host who charmed many people. His good reputation gradually spread, and after his father's death, Tian Wen took over his position as prime minister of Qi.

In order to develop his own power, Tian Wen devoted himself to making an impression on a wide range of people, no matter if they were rich or poor, the lowly or the noble. Tian Wen treated them equally and well. Seeing that this was not enough, he made a record of every discussion he had, in order to better know the person's family background. He would then send his servants to present gifts to the family members of his protégés.

One night, at a banquet Tian Wen was hosting, one person sat eating in the dark, and another man thought different food was being served to different guests and grew angry. He stood up abruptly and said goodbye to Tian Wen. Tian Wen, upon learning the reason, hurried to show the man his own plate. When the man realized they were all eating the same food, he felt so ashamed that he committed suicide. This story spread, enhancing Tian Wen's reputation for being hospitable. It was said that Tian Wen had hosted over three thousand protégés, among whom were men of letters, envoys, swordsmen, impoverished noblemen, even fugitive criminals and robbers. Pious people might have been ashamed of mingling with criminals and robbers, but Tian was of a different mind.

In the 25th year of the reign of King Ming of Qi (299 BC), after repeated requests by King Zhao of Qin, Tian Wen also became Qin's prime minister. The very first day he began working for Qin, Tian Wen's name was on everybody's lips. Some whispered to the king: "Tian Wen is a noble of Qi, he will put Qi first and Qin second, and that will be fatal for us!" The ruler thought this reasonable and put Tian Wen under house arrest.

On hearing that the king of Qin planned to kill him, Tian Wen dispatched a servant to plead with the king's most favored concubine. The concubine agreed but put forward one prerequisite: Tian Wen must give her a precious white fox coat — a coat worth more than a thousand gold pieces — which had been presented to the king when Tian Wen arrived at the palace of Qin.

Tian Wen, distraught, discussed this matter with his protégés. One of them, a former thief who could steal things by imitating the bark of a dog, said to Tian Wen: "I will get you the fox coat."

That night, he disguised in a dog's skin secretly entered the treasure house of the palace.

In this way, Tian Wen had the fox coat presented to the king's favorite concubine, who then interceded on his behalf and had Tian Wen freed.

As soon as he was free, Tian Wen and his retinue quickly left Qin. Just as they arrived at night at Hangu Pass, the last pass of Qin, the king of Qin changed his mind and sent a messenger to inform the guards at Hangu Pass to arrest Tian Wen.

According to Qin regulations, the pass gate could not be opened until the cock crowed. But how could a cock crow at night? Fortunately, one of Tian Wen's retinue could imitate a rooster. When he crowed, cocks all around followed suit. The guards thought it was time to open the gate, and thus let Tian Wen and his retinues through.

By the time the Qin king's messenger arrived at Hangu Pass, Tian Wen had safely entered Qi territory. Through the help of his presteges, Tian Wen escaped death, and after that, welcomed more people to his house, treating them well.

A man named Feng Yuan heard of Tian Wen's hospitality and arrived, wearing straw sandals, at his gate. He appealed to Tian Wen's generosity: "I have neither talent nor wiles. I'm here because I'm poor."

When Feng Yuan came to Tian Wen's house, the poor man was wearing a sword without a sheath, so he was housed with the lowest class of protégés.

One day, Feng Yuan sang a song while beating his sword on the ground: "My sword, go back! I have no fish to eat." On hearing this lament, Tian Wen placed Feng Yuan with the middle-rank protégés.

Several days later, Feng Yuan sang again while beating his sword: "My sword, go back! I have no carriage to ride in." On hearing this, Tian Wen placed him where high-ranking protégés lived.

A few days later, Feng Yuan sang for a third time, once more beating his sword: "My sword, go back! I cannot support my family if I stay here." Some people were disgusted, calling Feng Yuan greedy, but Tian Wen had his servants send food to Feng Yuan's mother. After that, Feng Yuan stopped his lament and devoted his life to working for Tian Wen.

Once Tian Wen requested that someone repay a debt. It was a difficult order, for many debtors were too poor to pay. Feng Yuan willingly paid for the man. Tian Wen had never met Feng Yuan face to face, and asked his aides who he was. They told him Feng Yuan was the man who used to sing "my sword, go back."

After that, as he was about to leave on a debt-collecting mission for Tian Wen, Feng Yuan asked: "Sire, do you need me to buy anything for you?"

"That's up to you. If there's anything you think I lack, bring it back," Tian Wen replied.

Feng Yuan then called all the prime minister's debtors together and calculated their debts. Then, he said to them in the name of Tian Wen: "You needn't pay these debts of yours anymore." He then ordered people to burn all their debt papers. These debtors all were deeply moved and loudly acclaimed Tian Wen's name.

When Feng Yuan returned, Tian Wen wondered why he had finished his work so quickly. He asked Feng Yuan, "Sir, have you collected all the debts?"

"Yes, master," Feng Yuan replied.

"What did you buy for me?"

"Before I left, you told me that I could buy you what you lacked. I thought it over and concluded that you have everything—treasures and beautiful women—everything, except virtue. So, I bought you virtue."

"What? Virtue? What do you mean?" asked Tian Wen.

"Sire, you just have a small territory, but you do not care about your people and collect usurious debts from them. In your name, I had them burn all their debt papers. As a result, they now hold you in high esteem. That is the virtue I bought for you."

On hearing this, Tian Wen could do nothing but say to Feng Yuan: "Well, I guess that is alright."

One year later, the king of Qi, jealous of Tian Wen, had him removed from his post. When Tian Wen arrived home, people came out of the city to welcome him—a truly moving spectacle.

Tian Wen then said to Feng Yuan, "Sir, today I'm experiencing the virtue you bought me."

Feng Yuan told Tian Wen: "The wily hare has three holes to his burrow. You must leave several loopholes for yourself. Now, you have only one hole, let me build another two for you."

Feng Yuan then lobbied the king of the State of Wei to appoint Tian Wen his prime minister. The king of Wei presented Tian Wen with one thousand gold pieces and invited him to serve in Wei.

On hearing the news, the king of Qi immediately changed his mind and asked Tian Wen to return. Feng Yuan told Tian Wen, "Sire, you can accept the offer, but you must require the king to build you a family temple on your land." According to the laws of the time, even a ruler could not violate those who possessed family temples. Tian Wen followed this bit of simple advice, and thus retained his honorable position in Qi until he passed away.

# Zou Ji, Music Maestro and Fine Prime Minister

During the Warring States Period, the ruler of the State of Qi, impressed by the counsel of the wandering scholar Zou Ji, appointed him prime minister.

No record of Zou Ji's birth and death have yet been found, but he was the prime minister for King Wei and King Xuan (356-301 BC) of the State of Qi. Originally a leading music maestro, his performances always enchanted his audiences, including the ruler of Qi, King Wei. The first time the king heard Zou Ji's music, he found he could not help but enjoy it, and decreed that Zou Ji stay at the royal palace. Not long after that, the ruler discovered that Zou Ji was not only a remarkable musician, he had a real aptitude for politics. Thus, the king appointed Zou Ji prime minister. It only took three months in the palace for Zou Ji to rise from maestro to prime minister.

This appointment annoyed the leading scholars of Qi, five of whom—Chunyu Kun,

Shen Dao, Tian Pian, Jie Yu, and Huan Yuan -- decided to interrogate Zou Ji to find out if he was really as wise as he was reputed to be.

Chunyu Kun put the first challenge to Zou Ji: "A musical instrument, while you hold it secure, is complete and can flourish. If you lose it, everything with it will disappear."

Zou Ji said, "I shall cherish your advice, and put it into practice."

Then Tian Pian said, "Pig grease is what enables an axle to turn. But pig grease cannot be used with a square hole."

Zou Ji said, "Sir, I understand what you mean. Obscurity lurks in the edges and corners to the right and the left. I should pay attention to the right and left flanks."

Then it was Huan Yuan's turn: "A fine bow is made of glue and wood. But the glue can do nothing to stop up the holes."

Zou Ji replied: "Sir, I know what you mean. I will encourage freedom of speech and attend to the common people's needs."

Then Jie Yu chimed in, "When a rare fox fur coat is old or ragged, a dog fur or sheepskin coat cannot be used either. Is that so?"

Zou Ji replied, "Sir, your meaning is clear. I must select talented and virtuous people to assist the ruler, and prevent crafty and obsequious people from gaining power."

Finally, Shen Dao said, "A big carriage needs to often be repaired, or it cannot carry goods; a fine lute needs to often be tuned, or it cannot play melodic music."

Zou Ji replied, "Sir, I will do as you recommend, and will reformulate regulations and laws to prevent officials from engaging in unlawful behavior."

After they left Zou Ji's home, Chunyu Kun said to his colleagues: "Zou Ji is an able man. We asked him five tricky questions, but he was never baffled. Before long he will be honored with a rank and title of nobility by His Majesty."

Sure enough, Zou Ji was made Marquis Cheng of the fief of Pi one year later.

It was said that Zou Ji was tall and handsome, yet one day he heard that a man named Xu Gong, living in the northern city, was much more handsome than he was. Once, while dressing before his brown mirror, he asked his wife: "Who is more handsome, Xu Gong or myself?" His wife replied without thinking, "Certainly, you are!" Zou Ji did not believe it and asked his concubine the same question. His concubine replied, "How can Xu Gong compare with you?" Several days later, someone visited Zou Ji, so he asked his guest the same question, and the guest, just as his wife and concubine before that, responded in the same way. Hearing their words, Zou Ji had almost believed he was more handsome than Xu Gong. Xu Gong himself visited Zou Ji soon after. Studying Xu Gong carefully, Zou Ji concluded that Xu Gong was indeed much more handsome than he. Zou Ji wondered: "It's clear that Xu Gong is better looking than I, but why didn't my wife, concubine and the guest tell the truth?" Pondering this awhile, Zou Ji concluded: his wife loved him, his concubine was afraid of him, and his guest wanted to flatter him. Zou Jin made a connection between this incident and the running of a state: For whatever reason, a ruler always receives one-sided reports, even faulty ones. If a ruler makes decisions and judgement based on these reports, it will bring calamity to a state.

The following day, the moment Zou Ji arrived at the court he told the king this story, as well as his concerns. Zou Ji concluded: "Today, Qi has territory thousands of miles wide, and a large number of cities and towns. Your Majesty, your wife and concubines love you, your subjects are afraid of you, people all over the country want to flatter you. It seems that you have been misled for a long time."

On hearing this counsel, the king thought it judicious, and announced that people were to be encouraged to report to him. At the same time, those who dared to point out the king's mistakes face to face would be given the highest rewards; and those who remonstrated with the king in writing would be given a moderate reward; while those who talked publicly about the court in the town would be given the least reward.

As soon as the order was announced, people all over the country actively offered their opinions, no matter whether it was at an official's house or in the marketplace. The king accepted people's advice and took real action to correct his shortcomings. One year later, some still were ready to complain but found it more and more difficult to find a reason to do so. The State of Qi certainly was not what it used to be, and growing stronger by the day.

Even after King Wei died and King Xuan ascended the throne, Zou Ji was retained as prime minister. In order to stabilize and develop the reforms being carried out in the state, Zou Jin recommended innumerable people of talent to the ruler. However, instead of being happy about this, the king was offended. On the other hand, another high-ranking official named Yan Shou found favor with the king, because Yan

Shou seldom recommended anyone to him.

Sensing a dangerous trend, Zou Ji said to the king: "Your Majesty, is it better for parents to have one or many filial sons? The same goes for a state. If all officials are like Yan Shou, what is best for the state and the society?"

Finding Zou Ji's words, made sense, the king changed his mind. He announced that the recommendation of able people was to be encouraged.

In fact, Qi had an admirable tradition for making use of various people of talent. Ever since the reign of Duke Huan, King Wei's father, Qi had set up a special residence for scholars called Jixia. Through this organization, Qi had attracted a large number of scholars representing different schools of thought. These scholars could write books, give lectures and discuss politics at Jixia. By the time of King Xuan, the number of scholars at Jixia had reached several thousand.

Through Zou Ji's untiring efforts, Jixia steadily gained even greater stature by attracting gifted people. The Qi ruler and officials at all levels became well known for treating those talented people very well. Many tales like the following were told:

Once King Wei of Qi and King Hui of Wei were hunting together. King Hui told his counterpart: "I have ten huge pearls that can light the way for twelve carriages placed one after another. Does Qi have such treasure?"

"No. We don't," King Wei replied. But he added: "We have something different. To my eye, a treasure of such pearls is most invaluable. However, talented people are my state's most valuable possession. People such as Tanzi, the man guarding our southern city; Panzi, the man guarding Gaotang; Qianfu, the man guarding Xuzhou; and Zhongshou, a man most skilled at preventing crime. They are all the national treasures of our state. Relying on them, no other state dares violate us, small neighboring states remain subject to us, and our whole state enjoys peace. I don't think your huge pearls can be put on a par with our national treasure."

Relying thus on its innumerable people of talent, Qi grew powerful politically, economically and militarily, as well as in other aspects of statecraft.

In the year 354 BC, when Wei launched an attack on the State of Zhao, Zhao asked Qi for assistance. Just as Qi's commander-in-chief Sun Bin, one of the most famous strategists in Chinese history, took up the challenge, a great idea dawned on him: he laid siege on Wei. As a result, Wei had to withdraw from Zhao the moment he got word of the assault.

As a learned person, Zou Ji was skillful at maintaining checks and balances on rulers. He actively persuaded King Wei to encourage officials and common people to put forward their criticisms and suggestions. Moreover, he knew how important talented people were for a state. Through his great efforts, many talented persons of his time were attracted by this farsighted policy and served the State of Qi well.

# Lü Buwei, More Speculator Than Prime Minister

In Chinese history, Lü Buwei's role as prime minister is seen as unique. He sought to become prime minister not to realize political ambitions, like others, but to gain title and honor.

Born in the final years of the Warring States Period, Lü Buwei was a very successful merchant. In ancient China, merchants might have been rich men, but they possessed a lowly social status. Lü Buwei, not being content with his wealth, bided his time, awaiting his chance to mingle in autocratic circles.

Once, while trading in Handan, the capital city of the State of Zhao (present-day Hebei Province), Lü Buwei met Yiren, sent by Qin as a hostage. Though Yiren was a son of Qin's crown prince, his mother—a concubine of the crown prince—had fallen out of favor with her husband, and Yiren had been sent as a hostage to Zhao. At that time Qin and Zhao were incessantly at war, and Yiren's situation in Zhao was precarious. Lü Buwei saw this meeting as an opportunity, as if his sharp merchant's eyes were feasting upon a rare piece of merchandise. He showed immense sympathy toward Yiren, at the same time speculating on the vast possibilities that had become available to him.

On returning from Handan, he asked his father: "How much profit can I make by farming?"

"Ten percent."

"How about through trading in jewelry?"

"A hundred percent."

"By assisting a prince to the throne?"

"More than one can imagine."

His father's words galvanized Lü Buwei's resolve. He quickly returned to Handan and told Yiren: "I know how to improve your situation."

Yiren smiled. "Sir, why not improve your own situation first?"

Lü Buwei replied, "Because mine depends on yours."

On hearing this, Yiren invited Lü Buwei into his bedroom to converse in private. Lü Buwei quickly gave this analysis of Yiren's situation: His father was the crown prince, and would soon be king of Qin. Then, he would have to select a crown prince among his twenty or more sons. Yiren, born to a concubine out of favor with his father, was a middle son. Even worse, he had been a hostage in Zhao for so long, he had had

no opportunity to compete to be chosen crown prince. The only opportunity he could make use of was that his father's favorite concubine, Lady Huayang, had no son. It was she who would choose a son to rely on, after her husband's demise.

Lü Buwei said: "I would like to offer you a large sum of money so as to influence your father and Lady Huayang to anoint you crown prince when your father becomes king."

Overcome with excitement, Yiren kneeled down before Lü Buwei. "Sir, if that day ever comes, I promise to share Qin with you!"

Lü Buwei then departed for Qin and bestowed money and treasure on relatives of the royal family. Through Lady Huayang's sister, he presented an array of pearls and rare jewels to the favored concubine. He also spread rumors that Yiren was virtuous and wise, and had befriended many important people in Zhao. Most importantly, he was said to sorely miss his father and Lady Huayang. Lady Huayang was most delighted to hear this. Lü Buwei had Lady Huayang's sister tell her: "A woman's beauty soon fades. Since you are the darling of the crown prince, why not choose a son as yours, and persuade the crwon prince to promise to make your son his successor when he succeeds to the throne. This way, when your husband passes away, or you are no longer beautiful, you will still have someone you can rely on. Yiren and his natural mother are not in the crown prince's good graces—so if you choose him to be your son and then get your husband to name him his successor, he will have to return your favor." Lady Huayang thought this idea sensible and thus persuaded her husband to make Yiren her son.

After that, the Qin crown prince sent money and jewels to Yiren, as well as found good teachers for him. Thus, Yiren gradually built up his reputation within the royal family.

While Lü Buwei was in Handan, he lived together with a beautiful dancing girl, Zhaoji, and made her pregnant. One day Yiren visited Lü Buwei and sat drinking with him. The moment he laid eyes on Zhaoji, he fell in love with her. He asked Lü Buwei to give Zhaoji to him. At first Lü Buwei was angry, but he quickly forced himself to calm down, thinking: if Yiren was such a rare piece of merchandise, why not invest more for an even greater return? Realizing Zhaoji could be very helpful in the future if she became Yiren's concubine, in the end Lü Buwei happily concurred with Yiren's wishes. At that time Zhaoji was two-months pregnant, but did not tell

Yiren. Strangely enough, 12 months later, she gave birth to a baby, Ying Zheng—who would later become the first emperor of a unified China, and become known in Chinese history as Qin Shi Huang. According to many historical sources, Ying Zheng was the son of Lü Buwei and Zhaoji. Regardless, Yiren remained under Lü Buwei's thumb.

In the year 257 BC, Qin attacked Zhao, and the ruler of Zhao planned to kill Yiren. Faced with such an extraordinary predicament, Lü Buwei paid out 600 *jin* of gold (worth a huge sum of money at the time) to bribe the generals and soldiers guarding Handan City, so that Yiren and his retinue could escape Zhao and return to Qin.

Lü Buwei told Yiren that he must remain an obliging son, filial to Lady Huayang. Yiren followed Lü's advice, thus strengthening his standing in Qin.

Six years later, Yiren's father became king of Qin, and Lady Huayang the queen, and as Lü Buwei had predicted, Yiren was made his crown prince. The next year, Yiren's father died, and Yiren soon took the throne, becoming King Zhuangxiang of Qin, with Lady Huayang and his natural mother being honored as dowagers. Thus, Lü Buwei had won big in his gamble. The new king appointed Lü Buwei his prime minister and granted large areas of lands to him. Like his father, Yiren soon died. His only son, Ying Zheng, actually offspring of Zhaoji and Lü Buwei, took the throne, and Zhaoji became the dowager. At the time Ying Zheng was still a teenage boy, and the real power was wielded by Lü Buwei.

Although Lü Buwei had gambled on helping Yiren become crown prince, he knew that people of talent were the real basis upon which a state flourished, and made sure such people were rewarded well. Li Si, who was to become the prime minister to Ying Zheng as the first emperor of a unified China, had also once been Lü's protégé.

In regard to politics, Lü Buwei insisted that the country should be united; as for culture, he encouraged people with different ideas to air their opinions. He made sure his protégés contributed to his book *The Spring and Autumn Annals of Master Lü*, where they told readers all manner of circumstances they had experienced or heard of. This book of 161 articles and over 20,000 words was completed in the year 239 BC. Lü Buwei thought the book covered all things under heaven, and ordered copies to be posted to households across the capital city, Xianyang (present-day Xi'an, Shaanxi Province). At the same time, he announced that those who could add or reduce one word in the book would be rewarded one thousand gold pieces. Although the book was hardly so comprehensive that words could not be added or reduced, *The Spring and Autumn Annals of Master Lü* remains an invaluable record of ancient Chinese culture, covering a wide range of ideas and philosophies including Confucianism, Taoism, Mohism and Legalism, and even topics like military strategy and agriculture. It is called the original book of eclecticism, a school of thought which flourished toward the end of the Warring States Period and at the beginning of the Han Dynasty.

Lü Buwei vigorously promoted the unity of the country, and for several years, the power of Qin was greater than the other six states that had survived the long years of war for supremacy. As Ying Zheng was still young, Lü Buwei was the real ruler of Qin. At the same time, he continued his affair with his Zhaoji. Thus, it has been said by some that Lü Buwei was not a virtuous statesman, but tyrannically abused his power.

As Ying Zheng grew older, Lü Buwei grew afraid of him finding out about his illicit relationship with his mother, and he sent another man named Lao'ai to become Zhaoji's lover. Lü

Buwei also deceived others about this, claiming Lao'ai was a eunuch. In fact, Zhaoji later had two children with Lao'ai, and hid them in the palace. Lao'ai then asked Zhaoji to make his son the crown prince after Ying Zheng's death. At the same time Zhaoji granted Lao'ai the title, Marquis Changxing. Gradually, Lao'ai became the second most powerful man in Qin.

Several years later, Ying Zheng took over the reins of government after attaining 21 years of age. Lao'ai grew afraid and launched a rebellion. Ying Zheng, who had known of the marquis' affair with his mother, had long hated Lao'ai with all his soul. Taking this opportunity, Ying Zheng killed Lao'ai and thus strengthened his power.

After discovering that Lü Buwei was the one who had sent Lao'ai to Zhaoji, Ying Zheng became disaffected with Lü. However, Lü Buwei still held the power after so many years and had built up a large network in the court. Lü Buwei was certainly the biggest obstacle to Ying Zheng implementing his own policies.

In the year 237 BC, using Lao'ai's rebellion as an excuse, Ying Zheng relieved Lü Buwei of his prime ministerial post and thought of having him killed. Finally, in consideration of Lü's great contribution to Yiren and to himself, Ying

Zheng ordered him to return to the territory granted to him in Luoyang (in present-day Henan Province), far away from the political center of Qin.

Over the years Lü Buwei had built up a great reputation among the other six states. The story of how he had helped Yiren ascend the throne of Qin had become legend. Many people visited him in Luoyang to invite him to work for the rulers of their states. On hearing this, Ying Zheng sent a messenger to Lü Buwei and told him: "What did you accomplish in Qin? Do you deserve the enjoyment of your lands in Luoyang? I order you and your family members banished to Shu as quickly as possible!" Shu (in present-day Sichuan Province) was a very remote place at the time, without proper conveniences and transportation.

On hearing this, Lü Buwei became very sad and angry. He remembered how he had made every effort to help Yiren become king of Qin, and of his intimate relationship with Zhaoji and Ying Zheng who was actually his son. He sighed: "When I picked up Yiren as a rare piece of merchandise, I had never imagined my own son would become my gravedigger!" Fearing a miserable life in remote Shu, he committed suicide by drinking poisoned wine.

Lü Buwei, in the vast span of Chinese history, is seen as more successful as a merchant than as a prime minister. However, though he may not have been the most virtuous statesman, his strategy for uniting the country certainly advanced the development of society and history. The book *The Spring and Autumn Annals of Master Lü* is most invaluable for studying the literature, different ideas and lives of people in ancient times. Lü Buwei encouraged different thoughts and views, and his contribution to the history of Chinese thought and culture is praised to this day.

# Qin Dynasty
# (221-206 BC)

# Li Si, the First Prime Minister of a Unified China

Li Si (?-208 BC) was a native of the State of Chu, in southern China. At that time, during the Warring States Period, China was divided into a number of independent states, constantly at war with each other to vie for supremacy.

As a young man, Li Si served as a petty official. He noticed that rats which inhabited the houses of the poor fed upon filthy scraps, and were constantly being chased and killed by people and dogs. Rats which lived in the barns of the wealthy, however, fed on the best grains, and were safe from harassment. ``It's the same with human society,'' he thought to himself, and there and then decided that he was going to better himself, and become a ``rat in a barn.''

He traveled to the State of Qi (in present-day Shandong Province), where he studied under the philosopher Xunzi. When he had completed his studies, he informed his teacher that he was going to seek his fortune in the State of Qin, far to the west. The young man had shrewdly observed that Qin was growing powerful through a series of progressive reforms, and was determined to unite the whole of China under its rule. Qin, he thought, would soon be the biggest ``barn" in the world. Xunzi approved of his plan, but asked him to be wary of acquiring too much power. ``When a thing reaches its zenith," the sage said, ``that is a sure sign of its imminent decline. When a thing reaches its limit, it turns into its opposite. That is a dialectical law of nature."

Li Si's arrival in Xianyang (present-day Xi'an), the capital of Qin, coincided with the enthronement of a new ruler, Ying Zheng. Through the recommendation of Prime Minister Lü Buwei, Li Si became an advisor to the young and ambitious Ying Zheng.

He told his master: ``All the other states are alarmed at the growth of the power of Qin, Sire. Their rulers are now busy seeking to form alliances against you." He then outlined a strategy of bribery and assassination to keep the other states at loggerheads with each other and to vie for friendship with Qin. The plan worked well, and soon Ying Zheng embarked on a series of conquests (230-221 BC) that was to make him the first emperor of a unified China. He is known to history as Qin Shi Huang.

Meanwhile, an incident occurred which

nearly caused the ruin of Li Si. An engineer from the State of Han named Zheng Guo came to Qin under the pretext of constructing a canal. Zheng Guo was soon unmasked as a spy sent by Han, which triggered a call from local Qin officials for the expulsion of officials who were natives of other states, including, of course, Li Si.

Li Si thereupon presented a petition to Ying Zheng, which read, ``The former rulers of Qin all appointed talented men from other states to assist them. As a consequence, Qin waxed powerful. Moreover, Your Majesty is surrounded by beautiful ladies and finery from all over the world. Would you be willing to forgo all these simply because they did not originate in Qin? Those who advise you to dispense with talented advisors are simply trying to weaken Qin and benefit your enemies."

With the Qin Dynasty in uncontested control of the whole of China, Li Si had achieved his goal of being a rat in the best-stocked barn in the world.

Qin Shi Huang enacted many important regulations and laws that exercised a far-reaching influence throughout Chinese history. Li Si was the mastermind behind most of these regulations and laws.

Li Si was an adherent of the school of ancient

Chinese philosophy called Legalism. As opposed to the Confucianists, who believed that human nature was basically good and that only the moral example of the ruler was needed to ensure social and political harmony, the Legalists believed that human nature was basically evil. As a result, strict laws and punishments were needed, the Legalists believed, to ensure peace and progress.

Under Li Si's direction, the empire was divided into 36 prefectures, each governed by a centrally appointed official. Li Si was also instrumental in standardizing weights and measures, the writing system and the coinage, as these had been substantially different in the different states. In addition, he started the building of the Great Wall as a defense against barbarian incursions.

However, there was also a negative side to all these laudable endeavors. Once at a feast, an official suggested to the emperor: "Your Majesty, it is most unwise to break with precedent. You should loosen your control of the empire, and grant lands to members of the ruling house, just as the Shang and Zhou dynasties did." When Qin Shi Huang asked Li Si's opinion, the latter was alarmed that ambitious ministers wished to break up the empire and return to the chaos of the Warring States Period. His response was swift and savage.

In 213 BC, with the powerful backing of the emperor Li Si forbade the teaching of history, and he ordered the burning of all previously published books, except for those on such subjects as medicine. Those who did not surrender their books for burning were tattooed on the face and sent to labor on the Great Wall. When scholars protested, Li Si had 400 of them buried alive.

Another episode that illustrates Li Si's ruthless nature occurred before the unification of the empire:

The greatest Legalist philosopher, and the man credited with founding the school, Han Feizi, had been a fellow student of Li Si. Han Feizi too was attracted to service in the mighty State of Qin, and Ying Zheng was favorably impressed with his wisdom and learning. Sensing a danger to his own position, albeit from a fellow student and fellow Legalist, Li Si moved to thwart Han Feizi's advance. He told Ying Zheng: ``Sire, this fellow Han Feizi is not to be trusted. He belongs to the ruling house of the State of Han. If you appoint him to a position at court, he will not serve Qin faithfully, but will intrigue in the interests of Han. However, if you send him away he will cause trouble for us later. The only thing to do is to put him to death." Ying Zheng was not entirely convinced, but, to be on the safe side, he had Han Feizi put in prison. While he hesitated whether to employ Han Feizi or not, Li Si forced his former classmate to drink poison, saying that the emperor had ordered him to commit suicide.

In the Qin Empire, only Qin Shi Huang was more powerful than Li Si, whose children had all married into the imperial family or had senior positions in the government. It was just as he was at the pinnacle of his career, that Li Si remembered the parting words of his old teacher. He noticed, also, that when the moon grows full, it does so only to shrink to nothing again.

In the year 210 BC, Qin Shi Huang traveled to Mount Guiji. He was accompanied by Prime Minister Li Si and the chief eunuch Zhao Gao, and his youngest son Hu Hai. At that time, Qin Shi Huang's eldest son and heir-apparent, Fu Su, was commanding a border garrison with General Meng Tian.

While still far from the capital, Qin Shi Huang fell seriously ill. Feeling the approach of death, he dictated a decree summoning Fu Su to hasten to Xianyang to supervise his funeral and succeed him as emperor. Before the decree could be sent, Qin Shi Huang died. Only Hu Hai, Li Si,

Zhao Gao and two other high-ranking officials knew of the emperor's death. Li Si swore them all to secrecy, scheming to set Hu Hai on the throne with himself ruling from behind the scenes. Both Li Si and Zhao Gao feared that if Fu Su succeeded his father, he would elevate his ally General Meng Tian to the prime ministership, and at the same time replace Zhao Gao as the chief eunuch with a member of his own faction among the eunuchs. They well knew that history presented abundant examples of the losers in such power struggles losing their heads as well.

Claiming to be speaking for the emperor, who, they said, was too ill to appear in person, they issued a decree ordering Fu Su and Meng Tian to commit suicide, on a charge of military ineptitude. At the same time, they announced that the new crown prince was Hu Hai.

When the forged edict was presented to him, Fu Su lost no time committing suicide. Meng Tian, however, was suspicious, and defied the order. He was soon put under arrest.

Hu Hai was the second emperor of the Qin Dynasty. But his reign was short-lived, prodded as he was by the callous Li Si to protect his illegitimate throne by ever-more-savage efforts to root out possible rivals until the dynasty collapsed in a welter of blood.

Hu Hai had his twelve brothers executed in

the marketplace in Xianyang, and his ten sisters maimed so that they could not marry and produce offspring who might challenge him or his successors for power. Countless others were slain for real or suspected opposition to the regime. Discontent spread, and flared into a series of open revolts.

The general atmosphere of terror and insecurity finally crept into the imperial palace itself, where Zhao Gao and Li Si had been content to share influence over the emperor. Now the two started to plot against each other. Each whispered in Hu Hai's ear: "Only we three know how you became the emperor. If the other reveals the secret, the people will rise up against you. It would be far safer to eliminate him."

Finally, the emperor heeded Zhao Gao, probably because he was a eunuch and could not found a dynasty. Li Si's family, on the other hand, was large and powerful, and possibly had their eyes on the Dragon Throne.

In 208 BC, Li Si was publicly executed, and his clan was exterminated. Two years later, the Qin Dynasty fell.

Li Si's burning ambition and the ruthlessness preached by his Legalist philosophy helped unite China for the first time. But these uncompromising qualities sowed the seeds not only of his own destruction, but of that of the dynasty he had served.

# Han Dynasty
# (206 BC-220 AD)

# Xiao He, Who Helped Liu Bang Establish the Han Dynasty

When you visit Beijing, residents may invite you to watch Peking Opera. One of the most famous Pekin Opera routines, "Xiao He Pursues Han Xing Under the Moon," tells a story about Xiao He, the first prime minister of the Western Han Dynasty.

Xiao He (?-193 BC) was a native of Peixian County (in today's Jiangsu Province). According to historical records, when he was young Xiao He earnestly imbibed knowledge of all the laws and regulations of the land. In the final years of the Qin Dynasty, he became an official of Peixian County. At that time, the founder and the first emperor of the Western Han Dynasty, Liu Bang, was just a village constable in Peixian.

Being Liu Bang's superior, whenever Xiao He passed by his residence, Liu Bang always invited him in for a drink. They soon became such close friends that whenever Liu Bang made an error in judgement, it was always Xiao He who tried his best to protect him.

In the first year of the reign of Hu Hai (the second emperor of the Qin Dynasty), Liu Bang was placed in charge of escorting some criminals. On their way to the prison, several criminals escaped, and according to Qin's laws, Liu Bang would have to be severely punished. So he freed the other criminals and fled into the mountains.

The magistrate of Peixian County heard this and arrested Liu Bang's wife, Lü Zhi. It was Xiao He who then pleaded for mercy for Lü Zhi, who was subsequently freed.

At that time, a rebellion led by Chen Sheng and Wu Guang had broken out and the entire country slipped into chaos. The magistrate of Peixian County decided to surrender to Chen Sheng, but Xiao He and his colleague Cao Shen disagreed, and suggested recalling Liu Bang. The magistrate approved of this at first, but soon changed his mind and ordered the arrest of Xiao He and Cao Shen .

Fortunately, Xiao He and Cao Shen were able to take shelter with Liu Bang. They then decided to attack Peixian themselves. Xiao He also wrote a letter to the people of the county and, because of his good reputation, obtained a positive response. They soon occupied the city and killed the county magistrate. Xiao He then supported Liu Bang as the new leader, himself becoming the chief consultant.

When Liu Bang pronounced himself against the Qin Dynasty, many others also rebelled across the country, including Xiang Yu who had launched a major rebellion.

In the year 207 BC, Liu Bang occupied the capital city of the Qin empire, Xianyang. While Liu Bang and his other followers lost themselves in the treasures and the beautiful women of the palace, Xiao He focused on gathering Qin's diverse archives. In this way, he grasped the whole situation facing the country.

Before his arrival in Xianyang, Liu Bang, along with Xiang Yu and other rebel leaders, had made an agreement that the first to occupy Xianyang would be ruler. When Xiang Yu arrived later at Xianyang, he disregarded this former agreement in order to try gaining military advantage. Liu Bang was absolutely enraged, and wanted to attack Xiang Yu. Xiao He, however, cautioned him, and said: "Sir, you are not yet strong enough to defeat Xiang Yu. Let us gather our forces and bide our time."

Liu Bang accepted Xiao He's advice and asked Xiang Yu to grant him the territory of Hanzhong (in today's Shaanxi Province). Thus, Liu Bang left Xianyang and stationed his troops in Hanzhong. However, since most of his soldiers were natives of southern China, some longed for their native villages and deserted. Among these deserters was a man named Han Xing. He was a truly gifted individual, but Liu Bang had taken no notice of him. Xiao He had observed Han Xing for some time, and realized the soldier could become a great general, which was what Liu Bang very much needed. Hearing that Han Xing had fled, Xiao He immediately gave chase. After two days and two nights, he caught up with Han Xing.

At first, Liu Bang thought Xiao He had fled too and was very angry. When Xiao He and Han Xing returned together, he accused Xiao He: "Sir, so many people have deserted, why did you bother to yourself chase down a common soldier like Han Xing?"

"Sire, Han Xing is no ordinary soldier. If you use him, he may help you establish a new state; if you do not use him, he will help others eliminate you. We are lucky we got hold of him before others could. You had better conduct a ceremony to appoint Han Xing your commander-in-chief."

Liu Bang then approved Xiao He's recommendation—though when soldiers found out their new Commander-in-chief was a nobody,

they were all taken aback. Yet when Han Xing displayed his talents to the full, helping Liu Bang overwhelm all other opponents including the powerful Xiang Yu, nobody dared to doubt Han Xing's ability any further. At the same time, people admired even more Xiao He's sharp eye for talented people.

In the year 202 BC, Liu Bang unified China and established the Han Dynasty, calling himself Emperor Gaozu. He appointed Xiao He as his prime minister and put him in charge of devising laws and regulations. According to historical records, almost all the prime ministers throughout the Han Dynasty followed Xiao He's judicial practices. As well, Xiao He was the main architect of the capital city Chang'an, today's Xi'an. He also organized the workers to construct the magnificent palaces and well-designed streets.

In the early years of Liu Bang's reign, the country remained unstable. Some still dreamed of establishing their own states, Han Xing being one of the main aspirants. Xiao He soon found out about Han Xing's conspiracy and, in the name of the emperor, invited Han to an imperial banquet. Soon after Han Xing arrived at the palace, he was arrested by soldiers lying in ambush, and sentenced to death not long after that. Thus, there arose from this a famous Chinese proverb *cheng ye xiao he bai ye xiao he*, meaning "The success or failure of an affair is all due to the very same person (Xiao He)."

One day Emperor Gaozu publicly rewarded the people who had helped him establish the Han Dynasty. Xiao He was put at the head of the list. Many generals were displeased with this, and argued with the emperor: "Your Majesty, we have fought many battles, while Xiao He has done nothing except juggle with words or express his opinions. Why is he ahead of us?" The emperor explained: "Ruling is much like a hunt. The hunter directs the dogs where to go. Your function is akin to a hunting dog, while Xiao He is the hunter. Generals, you are just commendable hunting dogs, whereas Xiao He has rendered the most invaluable service."

Yet despite Liu Bang granting Xiao He prime of place, as well as titles and lands, he still harbored some suspicions that Xiao He would one day seek to replace him. Xiao He, however, was most loyal to Liu Bang—or he would not have promoted Liu Bang's cause back in Peixian County in the first place. Learning of Liu Bang's doubts, nonetheless, Xiao He proceeded cautiously, sometimes acting against his own wishes.

Once when a general named Ying Bu had rebelled, the emperor launched the counterattack himself, keeping Xiao He behind to be in charge of logistics. Whenever Xiao He sent reports to the emperor, Liu Bang always asked the messenger: "What is the prime minister doing these days?" The messenger always told him: "The prime minister cares for the common people and is winning their hearts. He is now actively collecting food and money for Your Majesty." Hearing this, Liu Bang would often turn silent. From such queries, Xiao He realized the emperor was harboring suspicions about him. Therefore, in order to dispel the emperor's doubts, Xiao He tainted his own name by expropriating the fertile fields of ordinary people at low prices. In this way, he hoped the emperor would be led to believe that he had no ambitions for power, merely money.

When the rebellion was put down, Liu Bang summoned Xiao He to an interview. The emperor gloated, saying to Xiao He: "Sir, you are prime minister, how dare you take over ordinary people's lands? Look at these petitions!" The emperor thrust the letters of complaint at Xiao He, ordering him to deal with them. In this way Xiao He learned his plan had succeeded.

Perhaps sensing that 'to consort with a king is tantamount to living with a tiger,' Xiao He made arrangement for his own later years as well as for his family. He bought lands and houses in a remote place, so no one would have cause to be jealous of himself or his family.

As the prime minister of the Han empire, Xiao He served both Liu Bang and his son, Emperor Huidi. As he lay dying, the emperor asked: "Who should be your successor?" Xiao He recommended Cao Shen, with whom he had always had a contrary relationship. When Cao Shen became the prime minister, however, he did not divert from Xiao He's course but implemented his rules and regulations unchanged.

As the person who helped Liu Bang establish the great Han empire, Xiao He was the exemplary prime minister of the early Han Dynasty. In *Records of the Historian*, Sima Qian praised Xiao He as the greatest of all the high officials, a superb influence on later generations. "Xiao He Pursues Han Xing Under the Moon" is still a popular opera routine today.

# Cao Cao, Statesman, Strategist and Poet All in One

The first line of the book *Three Kingdoms* runs thus: "The empire, long divided, must unite; long united must divide." Cao Cao was born in the late years of the Han Dynasty, in 155 AD, when this empire, united for nearly 400 years, was slowly edging toward destruction.

Cao Cao, a native of Qiao Prefecture (in present-day Anhui Province), was originally named Mengde and nicknamed Aman. Cao Cao's father, Cao Song, was originally not a Cao but a Xiahou. However, as the adopted son of the eunuch Cao Teng, he assumed the surname Cao.

As a youth Cao Cao had loved the hunt, and delighted in music and dance. He was a boy who met any situation with ingenuity, being a regular treasure house of schemes and tricks. Once Cao Cao's uncle, outraged by his nephew's wild antics, complained to the father, who in turn reproached his son. The next time the boy saw his uncle, he dropped to the ground and pretended to have a fit. The terrified uncle fetched the father, who rushed to his son's side, only to find him standing, perfectly fine. "Your uncle told me you were having a fit," said Song. "Has it passed?"

"Nothing of the sort ever happened," responded Cao Cao. "My uncle accuses me of everything because I have lost favor with him."

The father believed the son and thereafter ignored the uncle's complaints, leaving Cao Cao free to indulge in his whims.

As an ambitious young man, Cao Cao secretly harbored high aspirations. Facing a corrupt and chaotic society, Cao Cao always worried about the future of the nation, hoping to change it one day.

Not having the benefit of an eminent family background, Cao Cao had to study hard, gaining a wide range of book knowledge, as well as mastering the martial arts. He also traveled far and wide, and encountered people with deep political convictions. Meanwhile, some people began to admire Cao Cao's talent and pin their hopes on him. Qiao Xuan, an official of the prefecture, once praised Cao Cao: "It seems the country is moving toward disorder. Only someone sent by Heaven can save it now. You are the chosen one, Mengde. I am old, and I would like to commit my wife and children to your care."

At the age of 20, Cao Cao became a petty official on the recommendation of two high-level officials who were impressed by his talent. Several years later, Cao Cao was promoted for his courage in suppressing a peasant rebellion.

The prime minister of the time, Dong Zhuo, was such an unrivalled master of prevailing statecraft, even the emperor was afraid of him, not to mention court officials. Cao Cao, together with some other officials, plotted to kill Dong Zhuo. Unfortunately, the plan failed and Cao Cao had to flee the capital, heading for Qiao, the district where he was born. Passing through Zhongmou County, however, he was arrested. Fortunately, the magistrate knew Cao Cao and admired him. And to Cao Cao's surprise, this magistrate, named Chen Gong, asked if he too could flee along with Cao Cao.

After riding for three days, and arriving at a place called Chenggao at a late hour, Cao Cao suddenly remembered that one of his father's friends, Lü Boshe, lived in a village nearby, and they soon found Lü's home. Lü warmly welcomed them and, entertaining them, quickly ran out of wine. After their host had left to get more, Cao Cao and Chen Gong had to sit for a good while. Suddenly behind the farmhouse they heard the sound of knives being whetted, and they overheard someone mumbling, "Let's tie him up and kill him." Cao Cao and Chen Gong both wondered if Lü wanted to kill them for the official reward. Going by the old saying, "He who strikes first prevails, he who strikes late fails," they killed Lü's entire family. They then discovered too late that the family had been talking of a pig to be trussed and slaughtered to feed the visitors!

After that, Cao Cao and Chen Gong left the village in a hurry. On the way out, they met Lü Boshe returning with the wine. The old man expressed surprise at their departure, but Cao Cao immediately killed the man without giving him a chance. Chen Gong chastised him: "What happened at the farm was a mistake—but why compound it?" Cao Cao replied: "Had he gotten home and seen his family dead, he would never have let matters rest. He would have certainly brought a mob after us, and we would have been done for." Chen Gong disagreed with him and considered it a great wrong. Cao Cao replied: "Better to wrong others than have them wrong me!"

This is the most famous story about Cao Cao, yet it might not be true. But many books of literature, especially the classical novel *Three*

*Kingdoms*, describe Cao Cao as one who would rather wrong others than be wronged. Here is a story that is considered true:

After his flight, Cao Cao came to his hometown and announced himself against Dong Zhuo. At that time, some other feudal lords also hoisted banners opposing Dong Zhuo, though each had his own reasons. Among them, the most powerful were the brothers Yuan Shao and Yuan Shu. By sending troops to fight Dong Zhuo, Yuan Shao and Yuan Shu both hoped to succeed Dong Zhuo. Although their joint forces won some battles, they could not kill Dong Zhuo. Most of these feudal lords then gave up and returned to their own territories. All, that is, except for Cao Cao.

On his way to pursue and attack Dong Zhuo, Cao Cao received word that Dong Zhuo had been killed by his adopted son Lü Bu. Cao Cao then went to Yanzhou (in present-day Shandong Province), where he gathered wise counselors and bold warriors around him. Thus, many talented people became his followers.

After the assassination of Dong Zhuo, the capital city fell into disorder. Emperor Xiandi of the Han Dynasty, hearing of Cao Cao's name, summoned him to the capital to take charge of the court. Cao Cao then hurried to Luoyang (in present-day Henan Province). When he found the city in a horrible state of ruin, Cao Cao had the capital moved to another city, Xuchang.

Not long after that, Yuan Shu, basing himself in today's Hebei Province, also pronounced himself emperor. Cao Cao was sent to attack Yuan Shu, and so began his effort at uniting the north of China. During this process of unification, Cao Cao had to contend with five main enemies: Yuan Shu, Yuan Shao, Lü Bu, Tao Qian, and Zhang Miao. Among them, Yuan Shao and Lü Bu were the most troublesome opponents of Cao Cao. However, with his talent for military strategy and the help of his counselors, Cao Cao took little time to defeat his three comparatively weaker enemies.

As a commander, Cao Cao observed strict discipline. Once during a summer harvest, people had fled when they heard Cao Cao's army was coming. In order to alleviate public misgivings, Cao Cao ordered those of his men who had damaged fields to be put to death. One day soon after, Cao Cao's horse was startled by an eagle and galloped into a field. Cao Cao immediately asked to be sentenced to death by a military judge. His followers, however, stopped him, and Cao Cao, in penance, cut off some of his own hair to show his adherence to the law. When his soldiers heard of this, nobody dared to disobey orders anymore.

Nonetheless, Cao Cao was still not powerful enough to defeat Yuan Shao. Yuan Shao had held the Central Plain for years, and possessed a powerful army and large territories. In contrast, his rival Lü Bu, though bold, lacked imagination, and was to become Cao Cao's first target. Through careful planning Lü Bu was soon eliminated.

Eventually a decisive battle between Cao Cao and Yuan Shao could no longer be averted. It took place at Guandu (in present-day Zhongmou County, Henan Province).

Faced with a more powerful Yuan Shao, Cao Cao still exuded confidence that he would win. Although Yuan Shao had the advantage in terms of overall strength, Cao Cao had other assets including his military talents, his trust in his counselors, his observance of strict discipline, his determination, and his indifference to slander. In the end, Cao Cao won the battle because of these very assets. The Battle of Guandu is a famous one in Chinese military history, where a weaker force overcame a stronger one. The battle, which lasted more than a year swinging back and forth, inspired many an interesting anecdote, the details of which may be found in the novel *Three Kingdoms*.

After defeating Yuan Shao, Cao Cao had become the most powerful force in northern China. In subsequent years, he eliminated the remaining forces in the north one after another.

By the year 207 AD, Cao Cao had become the master of the north. In the autumn of the same year, while passing Bohai Sea, Cao Cao was inspired to set down these beautiful verses that have been recited down through the ages:

*I gaze upon the boundless ocean*
*From Stony Hill on the Eastern shore,*
*Its waters roll in rhythmic motion*
*Surrounding islands in its mighty roar.*

*Although he lives long the tortoise wise,*
*In the end he cannot but die.*
*The dragon in the mist may rise,*
*Yet in the dust he too shall lie.*

*Although this stabled steed is old,*
*He dreams to run a thousand li.*
*In life's December heroes bold*
*Indomitable still shall be.*

The next step for Cao Cao was to march south, in hopes of advancing from victory to victory.

Jingzhou (in areas straddling present-day Hubei, Hunan and Henan provinces) was the door to southern China. Its ruler, Liu Biao, had just died before Cao Cao's army reached Jingzhou, and Liu Biao's son surrendered the kingdom to Cao Cao. By now, Cao Cao's plans were proceeding smoothly, and in accordance with his great ambition to unify the whole of China. Unfortunately, his plans received their first major setback at Chibi.

Like the Battle of Guandu, the war at Chibi is also remembered as a famous battle in Chinese history, where the weak overcame the strong. But this time, Cao Cao was at the receiving end.

Cao Cao's failure at Chibi could be attributed to several causes. First, the timing was off. Although the north had been united, some small rebel forces still fostered instability. As well, Cao Cao's troops had been fighting for several years, with no time to rest. Second, most of Cao Cao's soldiers were natives of the north and unfamiliar with fighting on the water. Third, after successive victories in the north, Cao Cao had become overconfident; while his opponents, Sun Quan and Liu Bei, were not as weak as they appeared to be. With the aid of the remarkable counselor Zhuge Liang, Liu Bei had gathered together great resources, and Sun Quan had gained mastery over the area east of the Yangtze River for years and his troops were skillful waterborne troops.

There were other reasons as well. Thus the Battle of Chibi resulted in a battle for supremacy. Cao Cao returned to the north and set about preparing for the day when he would unify the whole country.

As an outstanding strategist as well as a statesman, Cao Cao paid careful attention to productivity. He practiced a system of using garrisoned troops or peasants to cultivate wasteland so as to grow staple foods. In this way, the common people could lead stable lives and the army would have enough supplies. After a few years, agricultural production in the north recovered and developed.

After his failure in Chibi, Cao Cao realized that he should attract more people of talent in order to attain his goal of unification. He ordered that talented people at all levels of the society be enlisted to serve. This was a very daring step in Cao Cao's time. In the late Han Dynasty, only the sons of officials and aristocratic families generally had the privilege of becoming officials.

That is to say, those who had no eminent family background had little opportunity to have their talents utilized. When Cao Cao's orders were announced, gifted people born to poor families applied in large numbers to become officials, while many officials and aristocrats strongly opposed this policy. Cao Cao ignored the latter's entreaties and persisted with his policy.

Some important counselors of Cao Cao's, such as Guo Jia and Xun Yu, were born to poor families. Then there were those like Chen Lin, who despite having once been his enemy, was placed by Cao Cao in a key position after surrendering.

Cao Cao observed strict discipline by severely punishing the guilty and generously rewarding the virtuous. Cao Cao liked to dress casually when meeting his subordinates, whom he also liked to talk and laugh with. Cao Cao believed in the adage: "If you employ a man, don't suspect him; if you suspect him, don't employ him." Once someone told him that Mao Jie had spoken ill of him and then suggested Cao Cao should investigate the man. Cao Cao replied: "How can I suspect a subordinate every time someone informs on him?"

Cao Cao had several sons, among whom Cao Zhi was the smartest. At first, Cao Cao considered Cao Zhi his appropriate successor. But he later changed his mind because of Cao Zhi's disorderly behavior and unruly character. He selected another son, Cao Pi, who would strictly enforce his policies.

Cao Cao is also considered a great man of letters in Chinese history. According to historical records, Cao Cao was gifted in many ways, including being expert in calligraphy and chess, and skilled in medicine. As a great poet, he left to posterity beautiful verses. At the same time, he made great contributions to the genre known as "Jian'an Literature." Seven of the most famous men of letters during the reign of Jian'an, with the exception of Kong Rong, were subordinates of Cao Cao. Cao Cao proposed a simple and clear style, enunciating true feeling. It was under his influence and encouragement that 'Jian'an Literature' was created.

Cao Cao also showed great respect for people skilled in other fields, such as the sciences, technology, and medicine. After a few years, many capable people had gathered at Cao Cao's side.

In those same years, Liu Bei occupied today's Sichuan and Hubei, while Sun Quan continued to increase his power east of the Yangtze River.

Sun Quan wanted to make use of Cao Cao's strength so as to eliminate Liu Bei and was willing to become a subject of Cao Cao's. He presented a report to Cao Cao suggesting that Cao Cao proclaim himself emperor. Cao Cao said to his trusted followers: "I would not do that even if the time were right. I will leave this choice to my son." Until his death, Cao Cao remained prime minister of the Han Dynasty, although he wielded the power of an emperor.

In his later years, Cao Cao launched several attacks on the south, but with the tripartite balance of power, the task for unification became even more difficult.

In the year 220 AD, the 25th year of the Jian'an reign period of Emperor Xiandi, Cao Cao knew he was dying and wrote down his last words. He ordered his family members to bury him in a simple way and to maintain his policies even after his death.

Cao Cao is remembered as an influential man of politics and literature in Chinese history. Many of the stories about him retain their popularity even today, especially in the opera routines like "The Capture and Release of Cao Cao," depicting the saga of Chen Gong and Cao Cao.

# Three Kingdoms Period
# (220-265)

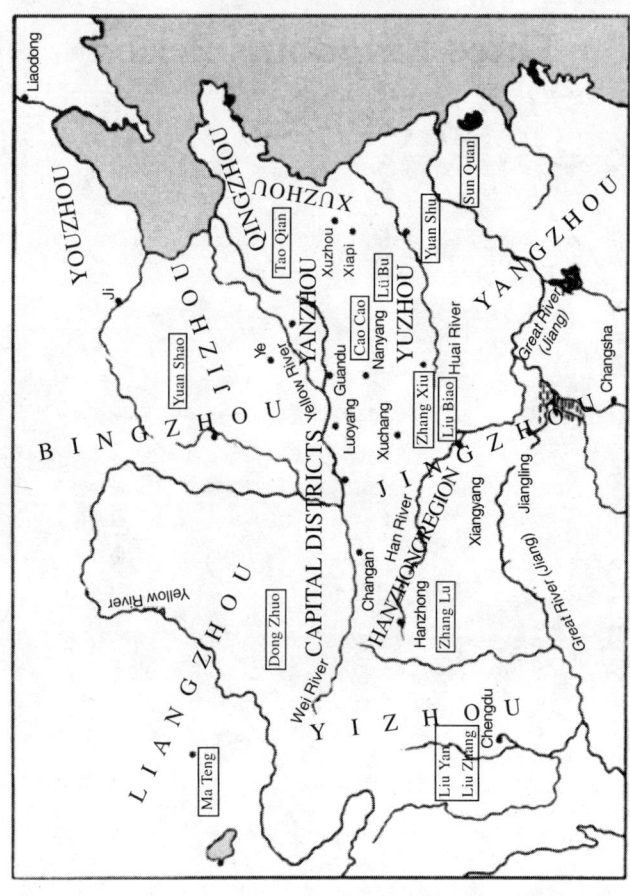

Provinces (*zhou*), districts and towns, and military leaders at the end of the Han Dynasty. The leaders' names appear in boxes.

# Zhuge Liang the Mastermind

Zhuge Liang was one of the most distinguished of the prime ministers of ancient China. Stories, sayings and legends about him still abound today. As a famous statesman and strategist, he is seen not only as a prime minister devoted to his state, but also a repository of wisdom.

Born to an official family in 181 AD, Zhuge Liang (181-234), also named Kongming, witnessed a world in chaos from early in life, when, at the age of four, a full-blown peasant uprising, the Yellow Turban Rebellion, broke out. Although the rebellion was put down by the government, it was a fatal blow aimed at the power of the Eastern Han. After that, the central government lost control of local administration, while local governors across China took the opportunity to expand their own lands and powers. Some became "local emperors" in the areas they occupied. Among these feudal lords, the most powerful were: Cao Cao and Yuan Shao in northern China, Liu Biao in today's Hunan and Hubei provinces, Sun Ce and his brother Sun Quan to the southeast of the Yangtze River, and Liu Zhang in today's Sichuan, Yunnan and Guizhou provinces.

At the age of seventeen, Zhuge Liang settled down in Longzhong (west of today's Xiangyang, Hubei Province), under the jurisdiction of Liu Biao. He lived there for ten years before he set out on his political career. Over these ten years, Zhuge Liang carefully studied the Confucian classics and other historical works. On the one hand, he learned a great deal from historical figures and events; on the other, he observed current affairs. He gradually developed his own political views and aspirations.

According to *Records of the Historian*, Zhuge Liang was a brilliant scholar with great ambition. He often compared himself to the famous prime minister Guan Zhong of the Spring and Autumn Period, and to General Yue Yi of the Warring States Period. Zhuge Liang, it is said, was self-assured about his abilities, and just bade his time awaiting a comparable leader. He chose to live a nearly recluse life, with only a few close friends, who being aware of his genius held him in the highest esteem.

When Zhuge Liang grew older, he liked to visit eminent scholars living in Jingzhou. Among them was a man named Huang Chengyan who liked Zhuge Liang very much.

One day, he said to Zhuge Liang, "I hear you are not married. You know, I have a daughter, who may not be beautiful but she is very talented. I think you two are well matched. Will you think about it?" Zhuge Liang replied, "I would be honored."

Huang's daughter was indeed a virtuous and talented wife. She turned out to be of immense help in the future. At that time of their marriage, however, she was regarded as unexceptional. According to some records, Zhuge Liang was a very handsome man while Huang's daughter was relatively ugly. A folk song is said to have offered this advice: "Don't try Kongming's way of choosing a spouse for life, because what you'd get is an ugly wife."

As his contacts deepened with other famous scholars, more and more people learned of his brilliance, some calling him a "sleeping dragon." In China, the dragon is a symbol of supremacy.

Zhuge Liang decided that the local governor Liu Biao and many of the other feudal lords of his time were not worth working for. He decided to watch and wait for the right leader.

The period was one of great changes: Cao Cao had defeated some feudal lords, unifying most of northern China; to the south, Sun Quan had grown much more powerful than ever before; as for Liu Biao and Liu Zhang, although they ruled a large territory in central and southwestern China, they did not have much of a future.

At the time, a man named Liu Bei was considered a potential challenger, though still not as powerful as Cao Cao, Sun Quan or even many of the other smaller feudal lords. As a scion of the Han royal family, Liu Bei embarked on a campaign to restore the Han Dynasty to its original splendor. Although the country was in chaos, emperor of the Eastern Han Dynasty was still the nominal ruler. From this point of view, Liu Bei represented a legitimate claim to the throne, whereas Cao Cao, Sun Quan and some others were in rebellion against the Han Dynasty.

Unfortunately, Liu Bei was never given the chance to prove his worth. While Cao Cao had united northern China and Sun Quan was in control of the southeastern Yangtze River valley, Liu Bei only possessed a small domain in Jingzhou, not far from where Zhuge Liang lived. Well known for his compassionate nature, Liu Bei's assistance was sought out by some famous scholars in Jingzhou. Xu Shu, one of Zhuge Liang's close friends, also became an advisor to Liu Bei.

There was a saying extant in Jingzhou at the time: "With the help either of the 'Sleeping Dragon' or the 'Little Phoenix,' you will rule the country." Xu Shu was the 'Little Phoenix.' Cao Cao heard this and took Xu Shu's mother hostage. Since Xu Shu was a dutiful son, he had no choice but to say goodbye to Liu Bei and go over to Cao Cao's faction. Yet, throughout his life, he never really served Cao Cao. A saying from this story is still in popular use today: "He who stays on Cao Cao's side but has his heart with the Han (on Liu Bei's side)."

Xu Shu was so distressed at having to leave Liu Bei, when he departed he recommended Zhuge Liang to Liu Bei, saying: "Sir, Kongming is a genius. If you ask him to work for you, you will realize your goals. Right now he is living in Longzhong awaiting the right master. But you must first demonstrate your sincerity to him." Liu Bei thanked Xu Shu, though he was also reluctant to see him leave.

Several days later, Liu Bei called on his two sworn brothers Guan Yu and Zhang Fei so as to go visit Zhuge Liang together.

When they arrived at the thatched cottage where Zhuge Liang and his family lived, they were told that Zhuge Liang had gone to a friend's home and would not be back for some time. One month later, Liu Bei once more asked his two sworn brothers to accompany him to visit Zhuge Liang.

Zhang Fei was most unhappy to do this, and said, "Elder Brother, I don't know why we have to visit this Zhuge Liang with such formality. If you really need him, I will bring him to you."

Liu Bei replied, "Mr. Kongming is a man of great learning. We must show great respect to him. If you are rude to him, I shall punish you." But yet again, they still were unable to meet Zhuge Liang.

In October of the year 207, when Liu Bei visited Zhuge Liang for a third time, they finally met. A memorable meeting it was for both of them. To Liu Bei's surprise, Zhuge Liang not only knew the full situation in the country, but he also predicted the tripartite balance of power in the future.

Kongming told Liu Bei: "Cao Cao is the master of northern China and the emperor is under his control. It is impossible to fight against him, given your present situation. Sun Quan, on the other hand, together with his father and elder brother, have ruled the east of the Yangtze River valley for several years. He has superior military strength as well as a natural defense—the Yangtze River. Our best choice is to unite with him. Now, the territories you have a chance of obtaining are Liu Biao's Jingzhou—and Liu Zhang's Yizhou (mainly in today's Sichuan). Liu Biao and Liu Zhang are all cruel rulers. I don't think it will be difficult to eliminate them. After that, you should clear politics within your domain, pacify the minority groups in the western and southern areas, and unite with Sun Quan. When the time is right, you should dispatch your generals to seize Luoyang, and you yourself should try to occupy Chang'an, the capital city. If that comes to pass, you will realize your ambitions and the declining Han Dynasty will be restored!"

This is a famous declaration in Chinese history, and is called "Questions and Answers in Longzhong on measures for unifying the country." Even now, high school students in China have to learn its written form in class.

Hearing this, Liu Bei grew most confident, saying to Kongming: "Sir, your words have really enlightened me. You are the most talented person I've ever met. Without your help, I will never achieve this great goal. I beg you join with me."

Zhuge Liang had long heard of Liu Bei's good character and was touched by his forthrightness. He agreed to work with Liu Bei, and thereby ended his life as a recluse. And so Zhuge Liang stepped up onto the political stage. He was only 27 years old.

For the following 30 years, Zhuge Liang served Liu Bei and then his son Liu Chan heart and soul. The situation really did turn out as he had predicted, except for the ending. It almost seemed that Zhuge Liang was a god who knew what would take place in the future. Yet he was most certainly not a god, though his wisdom was truly extraordinary.

When Liu Bei visited Zhuge Liang, he had an army of just several thousand soldiers. With Zhuge Liang's help, the troops under his command increased, and also won some important victories over Cao Cao. After eight years of preparation, Liu Bei finally gathered enough strength to realize his goal. As Liu Bei often told his followers: "Kongming and I are like a fish and water."

Still, Liu Bei was not strong enough to fight both Cao Cao and Sun Quan, for he still had no territory of his own. He was still under Liu Biao's suzerainty.

In the fall of 208, Cao Cao launched an attack on Liu Biao. Liu Biao had just died and his son soon surrendered to Cao Cao. At that time, it was impossible for Liu Bei to fight Cao Cao's one hundred thousand troops, so he had to flee to Xiakou (now Wuhan, in Hubei Province).

Cao Cao had planned to eliminate several small feudal lords such as Liu Biao and Liu Bei, and more importantly, the ruler east of the Yangtze River, Sun Quan. If he could do this he would unite almost the whole country. The feudal lords remaining would offer little resistance.

Considering his superior military power over Sun Quan, Cao Cao was confident of an overwhelming victory.

Zhuge Liang told Liu Bei: "Sir, Sun Quan and his family have ruled the east of the Yangtze River for two generations. I don't think he will surrender to Cao Cao. We must unite with Sun Quan. I can accomplish this myself. This is our best chance. " Liu Bei agreed without any hesitation.

Zhuge Liang then went to see Sun Quan alone.

At Sun Quan's court, two tendencies had arisen. One side expressed a call for surrender, while the other side insisted on fighting on against Cao Cao. Sun Quan did not want to surrender, but he felt that the possibility for victory was remote. With reasoned analysis, Zhuge Liang convinced Sun Quan that if he united with Liu Bei, they would both gain great advantage. Thus, an alliance was forged.

At the time, Cao Cao had stationed his troops in Chibi (in present-day Hubei Province). This famous war in Chinese history is therefore called the Battle of Chibi.

Most of the soldiers in Cao Cao's camp were natives of northern China, and they were not skilled at fighting on the water as southerners were. In order to prevent seasickness, Cao Cao had all their ships connected with huge iron chains. Zhuge Liang noticed this, and in discussion with Sun Quan's field commander Zhou Yu decided to resort to the use of fire.

On a windy night, Zhou Yu had one of his generals, Huang Gai, surrender to Cao Cao. Huang Gai then sailed ten big ships toward Cao Cao's ships. Filled to the brim with flammable materials for firing on the other ships, Huang Gai gave the order to set the fires when they were close enough alongside Cao Cao's fleet. These ten burning ships then set Cao Cao's whole fleet afire. Since all the ships had been joined together, breaking away was impossible. Cao Cao had no other choice but to flee overland as quickly as possible.

After this battle, the situation shifted just as Zhuge Liang had predicted. Cao Cao returned to the north, Sun Quan strengthened his position to the east of the Yangtze River, and Liu Bei occupied Jingzhou. A tripartite balance of power emerged for the first time.

After the Battle of Chibi in the year 221, Liu Bei quickly developed his fighting forces with Zhuge Liang's help. The most decisive battle was Liu Bei's occupation of Yizhou. It proved that Liu Bei could confront both Cao Cao and Sun Quan.

Beyond his military expertise, Zhuge Liang was also outstanding in running state affairs. When they entered Chengdu, Zhuge Liang enacted a series of laws and regulations. As a result, decaying Yizhou turned strong and prosperous.

Although Zhuge Liang had drawn up the perfect blueprint for Liu Bei, it required success every step of the way. Unfortunately, in its implementation, the plan went astray due to some individuals, such as the great general Guan Yu, who lost both Jingzhou and his own life. Even worse, Liu Bei, in attempting to avenge Guan Yu, made further mistakes. Kongming's plan was then completely wrecked. Liu Bei, defeated by Sun Quan, died on his way back to Yizhou.

Indebted to Liu Bei for the confidence bestowed on him, Zhuge Liang continued to serve Liu Bei's son, Liu Chan. Unlike his father, Liu Chan was a great disappointment. Zhuge Liang had to involve himself in all state affairs, big and small.

In the following few years, Zhuge Liang launched six big battles with the purpose of overcoming the Wei Kingdom, set up by Cao Cao's son. But for many reasons, he was not able to realize his goal, and died while still in camp.

The great poet Du Fu of the Tang Dynasty declared his respect and sorrow for Zhuge Liang in his poem: "Before victory was won he died, which will forever make all heroes after him wet their sleeves with hot tears."

In Chinese history, Zhuge Liang has been an exemplary model of the devoted official and a symbol of principled wisdom. Many stories and legends have arisèn depicting his extraordinary genius. Here are three of the most famous.

At the beginning of his career, many people doubted his talent on account of his youth. When Cao Cao sent troops to attack Liu Bei in Bowang, Zhuge Liang for the first time became commander-in-chief. He assigned tasks to every general, and then to everyone's surprise, ordered the preparation of a victory banquet. Guan Yu and Zhang Fei asked Kongming: "Sir, we are all going out to fight -- what are you going to do?" Kongming replied: "I will guard the city." Guan Yu and Zhang Fei sneered and left.

In consideration of the terrain in Bowang, Zhuge Liang decided to use fire. His analysis turned out to be absolutely correct, since Zhuge Liang was truly someone who could work out splendid strategies to win victories even in battles a thousand miles away. Since his debut at Bowang, people who doubted his ability began to show great respect for him.

During the Battle of Chibi, Zhou Yu, Sun Quan's commander-in-chief who was jealous of Kongming's brilliant reputation, was on the lookout for a way to get rid of him. Using the excuse of a shortage of arrows, Zhou Yu asked Kongming to make one hundred thousand arrows for the troops in ten days. Kongming replied: "Ten days may be too long. How about three days?" Zhou Yu immediately said: "Are you joking? Do not jest at a time of war. Do you dare submit your pledge under military law?" Kongming replied: "Certainly. If I fail to fulfil my promise in three days, I will gladly submit to the maximum punishment." At that time, it generally

took at least a month to make one hundred thousand arrows, so Zhou Yu thought that Kongming, even if he were a god, would this time have to face death. To Zhou Yu's surprise, three days later, Kongming brought back more than one hundred thousand arrows on ships. What had happened? Kongming had known that there would be adverse weather for three days. On the early morning of the third day, he had ordered twenty vessels, each with a crew of thirty people, to sail close to Cao Cao's camp. A thousand bundles of straw wrapped in black cloth were lined up on both sides of each vessel. Due to the thick fog and the river's dense mist, Cao Cao dared not advance in attack but ordered his archers to shoot at the vessels, just as Zhuge Liang predicted. In this way, Kongming instantly 'made' one hundred thousand arrows with ease.

Much later, the third tale took place, when Kongming was focusing on waging war against the Wei Kingdom ruled by Cao Cao's son. The commander-in-chief of the Wei troops, Sima Yi, was also a very intelligent soldier. Once due to blunders of a subordinate, it so happened that Kongming and a small contingent of 2,500 soldiers were stuck in a town, just as Sima Yi had managed to lead his main troops very close to the town. It would have been very easy for Sima

Yi to defeat Zhuge Liang if he had learned of his position. Everyone fell into a panic except Kongming. He ordered all flags and banners hidden out of sight and instructed sentries to execute anyone who tried to pass in or out of the town without authority, or anyone who raised his voice. Next, Kongming ordered the town's four gates opened wide; at each gate, a squad of twenty soldiers were to be disguised as commoners sweeping the roadway. After this, Kongming donned his crane-feather cloak, wrapped a cloth around his head, and followed by two lads bearing his zither, sat down at the gatetower of the town wall. He propped himself against the railing in front of a turret and began to strum while incense burned. When the Wei army arrived, Sima Yi was puzzled and dared not proceed. Knowing Kongming to be a man of extreme caution, Sima Yi became suspicious on seeing the towngate wide open like this, and quickly ordered a retreat. Kongming had counted on this and had ordered his two generals to lie in ambush as Sima Yi withdrew. When everything fell into place as planned, the astonished officials praised Kongming's genius, saying, "The very gods cannot outwit Your Excellency."

These stories are only a few examples of the many legends about Zhuge Liang that are still popular in today's China. His life story is so fascinating it would be most worthwhile for all to learn more about one of the greatest prime ministers of all time.

# Jin Dynasty
# (265-420)

# Xie An, a Remarkable High-born Prime Minister

In present-day Nanjing, there is a famous alley in the city, Wuyi Street, where the two most powerful families of the Jin Dynasty—the Wangs and the Xies—once lived. As time went by, the common people moved into this alley. A poet in the Tang Dynasty noted down this transformation:

*Swallows once flitted over Xie's painted eaves in bygone days,*

*Now dipping down among these humble doorways.*

A prime minister of the Eastern Jin Dynasty, Xie An belonged to the Xie family. Coming from a powerful family background, Xie An was well educated as well as intelligent. When he was only four years old, already there were those predicting a promising future for him. By the age of 20, Xie An had gained himself a reputation as being highly gifted.

As Eastern Jin only had territory in a part of China, some states to the north established by non-Han ethnic groups, as well as feudal lords in the upper and middle reaches of the Yangtze

River, always coveted Eastern Jin. Scholars generally preferred seclusion to being entangled in politics, so prior to his forties Xie An chose such a life, enjoying the mountains and rivers with his friends. But as a scion of the most powerful family of the Eastern Jin Dynasty, Xie An was responsible for maintaining the family's influence at the court. So he soon had to change his lifestyle and set out on a political career, particularly after his family began to face a decline in power.

During the first ten years of his political involvement, Xie An fully proved his earlier promise, eventually becoming the prime minister of the Eastern Jin Dynasty. In internal relations, Xie An devoted himself to developing consensus with other key officials; externally, he strengthened the army and overcame many invasions by Jin's enemies.

At that time, Jin's biggest enemy was Qianqin to the north. In August 383, the ruler of Qianqin, Fu Jian, decided to attack Eastern Jin with a combined force of 870,000 soldiers. The only choice Eastern Jin had was to fight back. In order to show his resoluteness, Xie An sent many of his own family members to fight at the front even as many cowardly aristocrats ran for cover.

Qianqin had much greater military power than Eastern Jin. So even some brave generals began to lose their nerve. As prime minister, Xie An remained steadfast and calm. He even asked his generals to play chess with him. In this way, he hoped to keep his subordinates cool-headed. On the other hand, he gave them distinct and thorough instructions. The Battle of Feishui is remembered as a famous war in Chinese history, where a numerically superior and stronger enemy was defeated by a smaller and weaker force.

After the war at Feishui, the Qianqin regime was destroyed and the enemy to the north was split by dissension. Under such circumstances, Xie An took the opportunity to march north hoping to recapture the lost territories of Eastern Jin.

In 384 and 385, Xie An occupied six prefectures to the north. Eastern Jin then possessed more territory than ever before. If the ruler of Eastern Jin was resolute enough, it was possible to control the entire Central Plain.

But the Eastern Jin court comprised feudal lords and aristocrats who were in decline. Internally, many officials were sharply divided. The emperor preferred drink and dalliance with his concubines day and night, rather than dealing with state affairs. At the same time, he feared lest

Xie An and his family should go beyond his control. On the one hand, the emperor granted honorable titles to Xie An, but on the other hand, let his own brother, a cruel despot, wield power.

Under these circumstances, Xie An requested permission from the emperor to leave the capital on the nominal grounds of fighting in the north. Xie An did this actually in the hope of avoiding trouble, since he was already 66 years old.

Not long after this, Xie An died in office. Three days after Xie An's death, the Xies were stripped of their power.

It is to Xie An's credit that Eastern Jin enjoyed more than half a century of stability. Furthermore, Xie An went down in Chinese history as a virtuous prime minister and an expert military strategist.

# Southern and Northern Dynasties

# (420-589)

# Cui Hao, Han Scholar-Prime Minister for a Xianbei Kingdom

In the period of the Southern and Northern Dynasties, there were several kingdoms vying for power in the south and in the north of China. The Northern Wei, established by the Xianbei people, was the main kingdom in the north.

The Cuis in Qinghe were one of the most powerful families in the country at that time. The Southern and Northern Dynasties are remembered in Chinese history as dynasties that attached great importance to family background. Cui Hao, as a member of the Cuis, found favor easily at the court, though his becoming prime minister of Northern Wei was mainly due to his great ability.

Skilled at calligraphy, Cui Hao was a man of great learning, who studied all manner of books covering diverse schools of thought. Emperor Wudi appointed Cui Hao as mentor to the crown prince. In 409 AD, when the crown prince ascended the throne as Emperor Mingyuan, he chose Cui Hao as his prime minister, placing complete trust in him.

Cui Hao initiated great advances in the military and cultural development of Northern Wei. As an expert strategist, Cui Hao helped Northern Wei win several key victories. The emperor praised him as "having knowledge of things long before they occur." He even proclaimed the following imperial edict: "In the future, the advice of Cui Hao is essential for anything concerning the military."

As a scholar born to a Han-Chinese family, Cui Hao was deeply influenced by Confucianism. Although he served at the court of the Xianbei, he had always admired the achievements of Han-Chinese culture and devoted himself to academic study. Unlike many scholars who were skillful at writing poems and articles, Cui Hao sought expertise in the study of systems, laws and regulations, and the Confucian classics. He delved into many books including *The Analects of Confucius*, *Book of Songs*, *Book of History*, and *Spring and Autumn Annals*. He also studied chronicles on astronomy and introduced a new calendar. It took 39 years for Cui Hao to complete all his studies and his treatises, making him the primary representative of the Heshuo culture.

Since the Xianbei were a people small in numbers before they established the Northern Wei Kingdom, they needed to acquire the advanced ideas and technology of the Han culture in order to occupy the Central Plain where the Han people had lived for several thousand years.

Cui Hao encouraged the Northern Wei emperors to promote Han culture within their territories and launched a campaign of "Hanification." His efforts greatly advanced the development of the Northern Wei. Yet most officials and aristocrats were from the Xianbei and ignorant of Han culture, and thus feared exclusion from ruling circles if Han culture ruled Northern Wei. As a result, many influential Xianbei people found cause to oppose Cui Hao.

In 450, Cui Hao was sentenced to death by the Northern Wei emperor, and his whole family eliminated.

Cui Hao, a tragic figure in history, was both learned and proficient. He made great contributions to the development of Northern Wei both in politics and culture. Unfortunately, a shortsighted ruling class hated him and sent him to his death.

# Sui Dynasty
# (581-618)

# Gao Jiong, Henchman of Sui Dynasty's Emperor Wendi

In the final years of the Northern Zhou Dynasty, Yang Jian, the future emperor of the Sui Dynasty, was the prime minister, while Gao Jiong, who was to become his prime minister, was his subordinate.

Yang Jian admired Gao Jiong's talent and personality, and considered him an able henchman. When Yang Jian replaced the Northern Zhou emperor and established the Sui Dynasty, he appointed Gao Jiong his prime minister.

Once, after Gao Jiong's mother died, as tradition dictated he had to resign his position to go into mourning for three years. Gao Jiong had stayed home barely two months when Yang Jian begged to return him to the court. Gao Jiong, in tears, had to refuse, but the emperor insisted: "I cannot rule without you. You must not say no to me."

Since Yang Jian did not rule all of China, there were some other smaller kingdoms still challenging him. In this process of unification,

Gao Jiong also played a key role. Among the enemy kingdoms, the Kingdom of Chen was the most powerful and prosperous. Yang Jian asked Gao Jiong: "Do you have any good ideas as to how to eliminate Chen?"

Gao Jiong replied: "Chen is located in a fertile region. We should first deplete their financial resources. Whenever the harvest is ready, we shall declare war on Chen. They will then have to conscript an army and ignore the crops. If we continue to do this, in a few years they will eventually ignore our declarations of war. The moment they do this, we will attack them. By then, Chen will have used up their resources, and eliminating them will be easy." The emperor gladly accepted his strategy.

A few years later, Gao Jiong and his army occupied the capital city of Chen just as he had planned. One of the Chen ruler's concubines by the name of Zhang Lihua was very beautiful. The second son of Yang Jian, Yang Guang, who later became Emperor Yangdi of the Sui Dynasty, asked Gao Jiong to bring Zhang Lihua back with him. Gao Jiong refused, which resulted in them becoming enemies.

Yang Guang was both devious and brutal. In order to become crown prince, he constantly tried to frame his elder brother, the crown prince

Yang Yong. In fact, Yang Yong was a very kind and learned person, yet Yang Guang made every use of his honesty and trustfulness to ruin his brother's name. The relationship between the emperor and the crown prince worsened. When the emperor wanted to disregard the elder in favor of the younger, Gao Jiong strongly disagreed for the sake of stability. But the emperor began to distrust Gao Jiong's advice since he was related by marriage to the crown prince. Hearing about Gao Jiong's aversion to him, Yang Guang's hatred of Gao Jiong deepened and he slandered him before the emperor.

After a few years, Gao Jiong lost the emperor's trust. When someone laid a false charge against Gao Jiong, the emperor found the excuse to downgrade his position to that of a commoner. In the same year, Yang Guang was anointed crown prince.

In June 604, Yang Jian, as he lay dying, discovered that the new crown prince was spending all his days with his concubines. The old Emperor was so enraged, and so full of regret, that he cried himself to death.

Yang Guang took over the throne and ordered the death of his elder brother, the former crown prince. In the year 607, Gao Jiong, together with other loyal officials, was executed by Yang Guang for defaming national affairs.

As a man of ability, knowledgeable of both civil and military affairs, Gao Jiong had devoted his life to the Sui Dynasty and helped Emperor Wendi build a stable and prosperous country. Unfortunately, he got inveigled in the imperial family's intrigues and became a victim of an imperial power struggle.

# Tang Dynasty
# (618-907)

# Wei Zheng, Mirror for the Emperor

Taizong of the Tang Dynasty is said to have been one of the greatest emperors in Chinese history. As the middle son of Li Yuan, the founder of the Tang Dynasty, Taizong, then known as Li Shimin, was a person of immense ability. He played a key role in eliminating the Sui Dynasty and establishing the Tang. He accomplished this by attracting many gifted and courageous people to assist him. He grew so powerful that even his father felt threatened by his ambition. When the Tang Dynasty was founded, Li Jiancheng, the eldest brother, became the crown prince according to custom.

Li Shimin, and supporters of his such as Zhangsun Wuji and Fang Xuanling, certainly did not just accept this state of affairs. In the year 626 AD, Li Shimin killed his brothers Li Jiancheng and Li Yuanji at Xuanwu Gate and forced his father, Li Yuan, to announce his abdication. Li Shimin then became the second emperor of the Tang Dynasty—Taizong, as he is known in history.

Zhangsun Wuji and Fang Xuanling were determined and efficient statesmen, though, in sharp contrast to them, the dry and humorless Wei Zheng (580-643) represented the Confucian moralist end of the political spectrum at Taizong's court.

Wei Zheng was a descendant of a minor official's family in southern Hebei, whose ancestors had served as petty officials under the Northern Wei and Northern Qi dynasties. At the end of the Sui Dynasty, Wei Zheng was a secretary on the staff of the rebel leader Li Mi. When Li Mi surrendered to the Tang Dynasty at the end of 618, Wei accompanied him to Chang'an. He was then appointed to the staff of the heir-apparent Li Jiancheng, whom he supported and advised in his struggle against Li Shimin.

Shortly after Li Jiancheng was murdered at Xuanwu Gate, Wei Zheng had an exchange with Li Shimin in which he displayed his extraordinary straightforwardness. When asked by Li Shimin why he had quarreled with Li Jiancheng and Li Yuanji, Wei Zheng replied that they had rejected his guidance on how to deal with their more ambitious (and now victorious) brother: "If they had followed my advice, they would never have courted disaster." Li Shimin decided that he could make good use of a man of such uncompromising forthrightness, and appointed him to his court.

When Li Shimin ascended the throne a month later, Wei Zheng was appointed imperial counselor and given a noble title. Soon afterwards, he was sent as Emperor Taizong's personal emissary to the northeastern plains, where he was to make peace offers to the remaining rebels. Wei Zheng was an excellent choice for such a mission, for he had himself been a one-time supporter of a major rebel leader. He could thus show from his own experience that former opponents of Li Shimin or of the earlier dynasty were not barred from service under the new regime. In addition to this sort of "diplomatic" mission, Wei Zheng was involved in other court activities. He was connected with several scholarly projects, participating in the compilation of a new customary code, the "New Ritual," which he and Fang Xuanling presented to the throne in 636; as well as being as one of the editors of the histories of preceding dynasties, compiled between 629 and 636.

Wei Zheng was rarely involved in day-to-day administrative and policy decisions, and it was not as a practical statesman that he became a symbol both for his contemporaries and for those in later times. Rather, it is as an unbending moralist and fearless critic that Wei Zheng has always been known—and indeed the Chinese have always regarded him as the most outstanding of Emperor Taizong's ministers. A memorial of 637 exemplifies the kind of blunt criticism that Wei Zheng often delivered. It was submitted in response to Taizong's inquiry as to how his later rule compared with that of his first years on the throne. Wei Zheng came straight to the point: "Long ago, before the empire was pacified, you always made righteousness and virtue your central concern. Now, thinking that the empire is trouble-free, you have gradually become increasingly arrogant, wasteful and self-satisfied."

Wei Zheng was a symbol of the deep mutual trust between ruler and minister, and the open exchange of candid advice that came to characterize the political climate of Taizong's court. His great reputation among scholars and officials of later ages surely derives from this role, so compatible with forward-looking interests and values.

And indeed, Wei Zheng played this role to the full. Here are some stories to prove it:

Once, Taizong's beloved son complained to him that some high-ranking officials above the third grade, including Wei Zheng, did not show him respect. To show his love for his son, the emperor resoundingly upbraided the court. Many ministers apologized out of fear. Wei Zheng, however, stood up and pointed out loudly: "According to the national laws, officials above the third rank should be treated exceptionally by the emperor. Even Your Majesty's beloved son cannot override these key ministers of the country, or national discipline will be destroyed. Emperor Wendi of the Sui Dynasty spoiled his sons and dismissed ministers from office. Eventually, he was assassinated by one of his sons and the Sui Dynasty was eradicated. Your Majesty, I don't think you should emulate Wendi."

Hearing this, Taizong was delighted. He praised Wei Zheng to the court: "All I was concerned about were my private feelings, while Wei Zheng was upholding national law. You should learn from Wei Zheng. He is a truly brave and loyal man."

Sometimes, even the emperor feared Wei Zheng's censure. One day, when Taizong was playing with a beautiful little bird, he saw Wei Zheng approaching. Afraid that Wei Zheng would criticize him for trifling with mere playthings and disregarding his loftier pursuits, he quickly hid the bird in his robes. In fact, Wei Zheng had already seen what the emperor was doing, but he had chosen to say nothing about it, discussing instead some other topic. Taizong found himself having to listen to Wei Zheng's endless talk, while distracted by preventing the bird in his clothes from revealing itself. By the time Wei Zheng had left, Taizong discovered the bird had died.

Although Taizong was one of the most successful emperors in Chinese history, in his supreme position, he sometimes could not bear when other people like Wei Zheng told him that he was wrong, and what he should or should not do.

On one occasion the emperor returned fuming to his residential palace, and grumbled to the empress, "One day I will kill that wretch!"

"Whom are you talking about?" queried the empress.

"Wei Zheng! He contradicted me in front of the whole court."

The empress said nothing but went into her inner chamber. After a moment, she appeared wearing her ceremonial robes, and said to the emperor: "Congratulations! Your Majesty."

The emperor was perplexed. "For what?"

The empress replied: "I heard that only a virtuous emperor has subjects who dare to speak bluntly. Since Wei Zheng dares contradict you at the court, you must be a virtuous emperor. Isn't that commendable?"

Hearing this, Taizong began to laugh, and then calmed down. He realized that Wei Zheng was a truly loyal official who would help him make the country strong, and avert the tragic fate of the Sui Dynasty.

So, at a banquet later that night, the emperor proudly told his officials: "Some say Wei Zheng is rude, but in my eyes he is excellent!"

Throughout Taizong's rule, the state was stable and people lived a peaceful life. According to historical records, crime diminished greatly during his reign. This period in Chinese history is called "The Flourishing Age of Kaiyuan."

Wei Zheng certainly contributed immensely to this period of peace and prosperity. He and Li Shimin had both been witness to the sudden collapse of the great Sui Dynasty. Wei Zheng pinpointed key social problems and offered analyses sharply critical of prevailing social evils. The emperor, knowing the basis of his criticisms, was happy to accept his advice.

Whenever Taizong went to Luoyang (in today's Henan Province), he always complained about the lack of sumptuous food. Wei Zheng heard this and warned Taizong: "Your Majesty, whenever the last emperor of the Sui Dynasty, Emperor Yangdi, traveled across the country, he always ordered governors to offer him local delicacies, on the threat of punishment. Since the emperor set such an example, this became popular with officials as well. This impoverished the common people even further and helped foster hatred of the emperor, hastening the end of the Sui Dynasty. Your Majesty, you should learn from this. Though you feel very secure now, you should guard against such excesses at all times."

The emperor was shocked, saying: "Only Wei Zheng can caution me this way."

With Wei Zheng's advice, Taizong implemented beneficial policies for the common people, resulting in a peaceable administration. This was not long after a period of war. Whenever Taizong compared the prevailing situation to the early years of his reign, he would say: "It is Wei Zheng who has helped me bring on this stability and prosperity."

Wei Zheng, being such a devoted official, cared little for his own health. When the new year of 643 arrived, Wei Zheng fell seriously ill. The emperor sent the best doctors to see Wei Zheng, and he himself also went to visit him. This, in feudal society, was the highest treatment an official could receive. When Taizong found Wei Zheng's house to be very dilapidated, he ordered a hall built for Wei Zheng with the materials normally used for building a palace.

When at death's door, asked by the emperor what his last wish would be, Wei Zheng was said to have replied: "I don't care about my own troubles—what matters most to me is the rise and fall of our country." The emperor was so moved that he broke down.

Emperor Taizong personally attended Wei Zheng's funeral. According to Wei Zheng's last wishes, he was given a simple burial. The emperor himself wrote an essay that was carved onto Wei Zheng's tomb. Wei Zheng's image is also seen among the 24 exemplary ministers enshrined at Linyan Pavilion in the imperial palace.

Emperor Taizong sorely missed Wei Zheng. He often told his officials: "We may put our cap straight by using bronze as a mirror; we may fathom the rise and fall of kingdoms by regarding the doings of the ancients as a mirror; and we may know our own errors and propriety by regarding the people as a mirror. I have always possessed these three mirrors. Now, with Wei Zheng's death, I have lost the most important of my 'mirrors'!"

# Fang Xuanling, Most Capable Aide to Emperor Taizong

Emperor Taizong of the Tang Dynasty, one of China's finest emperors, was able to attract people of excellent ability to work for him even when he was young. These people later became his most trusted ministers, with Fang Xuanling heading the list.

Born to an official family in the Sui Dynasty, Fang Xuanling (579-648) showed considerable promise when he was a child. More than diligent at study, Fang Xuanling was also perceptive and analytical. He always held his own opinions, which were representative of his great ambition, striking intelligence and extraordinary determination.

After long years of division, when the Sui Dynasty unified the country most people thought that peace and stabiltiy awaited them, but young Fang Xuanling did not agree. He told his father: "The emperor has neither talent nor virtue. Although he has unified the country, many of his actions bode ill for the future. I hear that in the royal family, brothers are enemies, and father and son have a hostile relationship. Everything may appear alright for now, but their days are numbered."

Hearing this, his father grew fearful and stopped him: "Children should not talk about politics." But his father also realized that Fang Xuanling was no ordinary child.

At age 18, Fang Xuanling passed the imperial examination and launched on his political career. His exceptional powers of observation and distinctive manner set him apart, and other officials soon noticed him, speaking highly of him. The official Gao Xiaoji, famous for selecting the best people, is said to have noted when he met Fang Xuanling for the first time: "I have never met anyone like Fang Xuanling. I should lose no time in recommending him to the court."

But Fang Xuanling's service during the Sui Dynasty was by no means smooth, and he was later even banished.

The second emperor of the Sui Dynasty, Yangdi, had killed his father and elder brother to become the new ruler. He was a very brutal and greedy man. So as to pursue a life of luxury, he commanded local governors to present him with the best food and jewels. The life of the common people soon hit rock bottom. Many officials and landlords also began to turn against the Sui Dynasty.

Fang Xuanling, realizing Li Yuan and his son Li Shimin were people he could work for, did not hesitate to visit them. Li Shimin, who later became Emperor Taizong of the Tang Dynasty, was a person of great charm. In intimate discussion with Fang Xuanling, they both expressed regrets over not having had the chance to meet before. Fang Xuanling soon became Li Shimin's most trusted counselor, and his advice greatly aided Li Shimin in consolidating power and building his reputation.

Fang Xuanling soon realized that the real basis of a court was the talented people it possessed, so he always searched for the best people to serve Li Shimin. Whenever they occupied a new city, other people rushed to grab money and jewels, whereas Fang Xuanling visited captured generals and disenchanted scholars, registering their names as well as treating them kindly. Many generals and officials of the early Tang Dynasty, including Xu Shixun and Du Ruhui, were directly or indirectly brought in by Fang Xuanling.

Later, when Li Yuan bestowed the title of King Qin on his son Li Shimin, Fang Xuanling took control of finances at Li Shimin's palace.

Over the following decade, Fang Xuanling built up a flexible, comprehensive and highly efficient administration. Li Shimin did not have to worry about domestic affairs, for he placed great trust in Fang Xuanling.

With the help of Li Shimin and his followers, Li Yuan unified China and established the Tang Dynasty in 618. According to tradition, Li Shimin's elder brother Li Jiancheng should have become crown prince. However, in the process of unifying China, Li Shimin had built up a remarkable reputation, even greater than his father's. Many notables were attracted by Li Shimin's name, rather than by his father Li Yuan, and certainly not his elder brother. Li Jiancheng was very jealous of Li Shimin and tried several times to secretly have him killed. But with the support of many astute advisors like Fang Xuanling, Li Shimin escaped death every time.

Although Li Shimin realized that the relationship between his brother and himself had turned lethal, he hesitated to kill his own brother. Fang Xuanling said to him: "Sire, while I can fully understand your feelings, you really have no other choice. Life or death, you must chose one." A plan was set into motion.

At Xuanwu Gate, Li Shimin attacked his brothers Li Jiancheng and Li Yuanji. During the fighting, Li Shimin fell off his horse and Li Yuanji almost killed him. Fang Xuanling swiftly sent a brave general to rescue Li Shimin just in time. Eventually, Li Jiancheng and Li Yuanji were killed by Li Shimin and his followers. The incident at Xuanwu Gate is a famous event in Chinese history

On hearing the news Li Yuan, their father, was most grieved, and now came under pressure from Li Shimin. He wisely decided to abdicate and hand over the throne to Li Shimin. King Qin then became Emperor Taizong of the Tang Dynasty.

The new emperor rewarded his most deserving officials with honorable titles and large fiefs. He also appointed Fang Xuanling and Du Ruhui as his 'right' and 'left' prime ministers.*

As mentioned before, Du Ruhui had been introduced to the emperor by Fang Xuanling. Even though Li Shimin did not know Du Ruhui at all, Fang Xuanling had insisted on assigning Du Ruhui to a key position. As expected, Du Ruhui turned out to be an impressive minister. The harmonious relationship between Fang

---

* In ancient China, the prefixes "left" and "right" were commonly used for officials appointed in pairs to one office, with "left" taking precedence over "right" in prestige.

Xuanling and Du Ruhui was a great asset to Li Shimin.

Whenever Li Shimin discussed state affairs with Fang Xuanling, Fang always insisted on asking Du Ruhui to join them. When Du Ruhui spoke, he often expressed the same ideas as Fang Xuanling. It has been said that Fang Xuanling excelled at strategy while Du Ruhui was perceptive in judgment. So as to pool their different strengths, Fang Xuanling made every effort to work in accord with Du Ruhui and bring their collective talents into full play. They laid down a model for later generations of how two gifted persons could work together.

Regarding his prime minister as his right hand, Emperor Taizong held Fang Xuanling in the greatest esteem. Outside their relationship as ruler and subject, Taizong and Fang Xuanling were in fact relatives. Fang's daughter was one of the emperor's concubines, and Fang Xuanling's son also married one of the princesses. At the same time, Taizong granted other titles to Fang Xuanling that would have established him at the pinnacle of power. Fang Xuanling, however, being a modest and prudent man, wanted to avoid any jealousy. He thanked the emperor but refused to accept the titles. Taizong said: "I know you are modest, but you deserve it. Please don't refuse."

Now Fang Xuanling thought it time for him to resign. He asked the emperor again and again to let him retire for the sake of his health. Taizong certainly hated to let Fang Xuanling go, but he knew Fang Xuanling was old and poor in health, and needed a good rest. At long last, Fang Xuanling was permitted to retire.

Even though he was sequestered at home, Fang Xuanling still paid close attention to happenings at the court. When Taizong insisted on attacking Gaoli (today's Korea), nobody dared rein in the excessiveness of the emperor. Fang Xuanling then said to his son: "If I don't stop the emperor, I will be letting His Majesty down."

He therefore wrote a report to the emperor, and had his princess daughter-in-law deliver it to Taizong. The emperor was deeply moved, saying: "What a loyal official he is! I heard he is seriously ill, but still he cares about the country."

Taizong ordered a path made from the palace to Fang Xuanling's house, so he could often visit his most trusted senior advisor. At the same time, the emperor requested the crown prince to visit Fang Xuanling every day. This show of respect was beyond the best any official could hope for.

At age 71, Fang Xuanling died quietly. Taizong had him buried in the imperial cemetery, while his son, Emperor Gaozong, bestowed on him honorary titles posthumously.

# Di Renjie, Prime Minister to the Only Female Emperor

Wu Zetian is known as the only female emperor in Chinese history. She was once the concubine of Taizong, second emperor of the Tang Dynasty. It was said that she was very beautiful and brilliant. Zhi was Emperor Taizong's son who began an affair with Wu Zetian, then his father's concubine, after becoming the crown prince. On Taizong's death, Zhi ascended the throne as Emperor Gaozong, and made sure that Wu Zetian became his concubine. Wu Zetian was a talented, ambitious and strong-willed woman, as much as her husband was weak and inept. Wu Zetian gradually became the real power in the country. Later, when her husband died, she brushed her own sons aside and declared herself emperor.

As the one and only female emperor in Chinese history, Wu Zetian faced pressure every step of the way, and required the most talented people to run her state, as well as to make officials and common people submit themselves to her rule. It was to her great fortune that she found Di Renjie.

Many officials prejudged Wu Zetian because she was a woman, but Di Renjie was of a different mind. He knew both the common people and officials were in need of a good ruler, and whether this was to be a man or a woman was not important.

Di Renjie (629-690), named Huaiying, was born to an official's family in what is now Taiyuan, in Shanxi Province. When he was a child he was very clever and fond of learning. He was eventually recommended to take charge of the administration of justice for the government in Bingzhou.

In the year 677, during the reign of Emperor Gaozong, Di Renjie was promoted to become chief justice. Within one year, he tried and passed sentence on more than 17,000 cases that had accumulated over many years. He always concentrated on investigation and facts and, most importantly, never twisted the law to suit his own purposes or to flatter anybody. As a result, there were no longer complainants seeking justice after his trials.

When a general named Quan Shancai carelessly cut down a tree at the Zhaoling Mausoleum (Taizong's tomb), Di Renjie wanted to punish him by relieving him of his post, as the state law decreed. But Emperor Gaozong was so angry he ordered Di Renjie to sentence Quan Shancai to death. Di Renjie disagreed and told the emperor: "Your Majesty, these laws have been enacted by you and disseminated to the public. The punishments must fit the crimes. How can we sentence a person to death when he does not deserve such a punishment? A thousand years later, what will people think of you?" Hearing this, the emperor calmed down and let Quan Shancai off lightly.

Another official, Wang Benli, was a favorite of the emperor. He often bullied other officials, and nobody dared challenge him. Di Renjie decided Wang Benli should be punished. Though the emperor tried to protect Wang Benli at first, Di Renjie stubbornly persisted. Finally, Wang Benli was punished and Di Renjie gained the respect of the whole court.

Stories concerning Di Renjie's investigation of cases are recorded by both official and unofficial history books, and are still popular today. A Dutch scholar has even written a book on Di Renjie's inquiries.

When Wu Zetian declared herself Emperor and supplanted the Tang Dynasty with the Zhou, she appointed Di Renjie her prime minister. Di

Renjie was so forthright that it is not surprising he offended a few people.

One day Wu Zetian asked Di Renjie: "You had a good reputation when you were in Runan. Do you want to know who criticizes you behind your back?"

Di Renjie replied: "Your Majesty, if you think I've done something wrong, I would correct it at once. Now, as long as you don't find me to be wrong, I am fortunate. Is there any necessity then for me to know who speaks evil of me?"

Wu Zetian was surprised at his answer, but full of admiration.

As the only woman emperor in Chinese history, Wu Zetian appointed many upright and gifted administrators such as Di Renjie to help her; at the same time, to maintain respect for the rule of law, she had to rely on the severity of certain officials. In the year 692, Di Renjie was jailed by one such official, Lai Junchen, famous for his cruelty. When Lai Junchen asked him if he would join their plot against the emperor, Di Renjie had said yes so as to avoid harsh punishment and save his own life. But when they tried to use Di Renjie to frame a case against one upright official, Di Renjie put his own head to the stone wall for showing his refusal. Lai Junchen was most taken aback when Di Renjie did this. The moment he got the chance, Di Renjie wrote a message on his robes, then asked for his family to wash them for him. His son took the clothes to the palace and gave them to Wu Zetian, who freed Di Renjie immediately.

When they met at the palace again, Wu Zetian asked, "Why did you declare that you were against me?"

Di Renjie replied, "If I had not said that, I would not have been able to meet Your Majesty again in this life."

On account of this incident, Di Renjie was demoted to county magistrate.

In the year 697, Di Renjie was reconfirmed as prime minister by Wu Zetian. Under Wu Zetian's coercive regime, many people did not dare to say anything and kept whatever criticisms they might have had to themselves. There was even an official who told his own brother that he had to tolerate whatever happened—even if someone spat on his face, he should just let it pass. Di Renjie, however, was different altogether. He feared nobody, always daring to tell the truth when needed.

After Wu Zetian set up her Zhou Dynasty in place of the Tang, she contemplated selecting a crown prince from the Wu clan. Her nephew Wu Chengsi had been actively canvassing her to become crown prince. Since this was a very sensitive issue, nobody dared to talk about it before the emperor. Even when some brave officials ventured to express their opinions, Wu Zetian always ignored them. Di Renjie, however, was an exception.

Whenever he had the chance, he spoke to the emperor about this: "Your Majesty, the officials in the court are senior members of the Tang Dynasty. They admire you and accept the fact that the Zhou has replaced the Tang. But if a member of the Wu clan takes the throne, I wonder what would happen. After all, the relationship between you and your son is that of a mother and son, while that between you and Wu Chengsi is that of an aunt and nephew. Who is closer?"

Wu Zetian thought his words reasonable and reaffirmed her son as crown prince.

As an incorruptible and intelligent official, Di Renjie knew his subordinates well enough to assign them jobs commensurate with their abilities. Once, two Qidan generals surrendered to the Zhou, and most officials thought they should be executed since they had wounded and killed countless officials and soldiers of the Zhou. Wu Zetian hesitated in making a decision, but Di Renjie told her: "These two generals are very brave and capable. Your Majesty, if you pardon them, they would most certainly remain loyal to you." Wu Zetian subsequently appointed them to be Zhou generals. In a later war against Qidan, these two generals performed bravely, just as Di Renjie had predicted, even capturing some of their former leaders alive. Wu Zetian was overjoyed and held a victory banquet in their honor.

At the feast, Wu Zetian herself raised a toast to Di Renjie and said: "Sir, full credit must go to you."

Di Renjie humbly replied: "Your Majesty, I do not deserve it. It depended on your great determination as well as these generals' courage."

Di Renjie realized that skillful people were vital for a country's development, so he focused on searching for good people with the necessary qualities for serving the court.

One day, Wu Zetian asked Di Renjie, "I want someone suitable for the post of prime minister or commander-in-chief. Can you recommend someone?"

Di Renjie replied: "Zhang Jianzhi, now the administrator of Jinzhou, is an able person. I wish he could be given an important position."

Wu Zetian called Zhang Jianzhi to the court, but she did not give him a high-ranking position.

Several days later, Wu Zetian again asked Di Renjie to recommend some talented people. Di Renjie said, "I recommended Zhang Jianzhi a few days ago. Why did you not put him in an important position?"

Wu Zetian said, "I have promoted him!"

Di Renjie replied, "I recommended him to be prime minister, not the position he is now in."

In the end, Wu Zetian appointed Zhang Jianzhi as the right prime minister. Some other notable people, including Yao Chong who later became the famous prime minister of Emperor Xuanzong, were also recommended by Di Renjie. Some said to Di Renjie: "Sir, you have been a mentor to many high-ranking talented people."

Di Renjie replied: "What I do is for the state, not for my own reputation."

Once Wu Zetian ordered the two prime ministers to recommend a Shangshulang, secretary of state. Di Renjie recommended his eldest son, Di Guangsi. As the father had expected, Di Guangsi performed his duties masterfully. Wu Zetian praised Di Renjie, saying, "Sir, in ancient times, Qi Xi recommended virtuous people notwithstanding his own relations. You truly rule in the manner of those ancient men of virtue!"

When Di Renjie died in 690, Wu Zetian cried out: "My court is empty!" In her eyes, all the officials in the court did not equal the singular Di Renjie. After his death, Di Renjie was lauded highly by both Wu Zetian and later emperors. Furthermore, tales about him are still popular today. Thus Di Renjie was able to win a name for himself not only in his own lifetime but also long after his death.

# Five Dynasties
(907-960)

# Feng Dao, Rolling Through Troubled Times

There is an old Chinese saying that goes: "A change of sovereign brings a change of ministers." In Chinese history, a minister might serve different emperors within the same dynasty, but it seldom occurred that a minister served different rulers of different dynasties. Feng Dao was such an exception.

After the great Tang Dynasty, China was divided into several kingdoms incessantly fighting for territory and power. Over a long period, five dynasties—the Liang, Tang, Jing, Han and Zhou—appeared one after another.

Feng Dao (882-954) was born in the late years of the Tang Dynasty (882-954). Lacking a prominent family background, Feng Dao studied very hard when he was young. He had hopes of joining the team of ministers in the future. In the year 907, a peasant army led by Huang Chao eliminated the Tang Dynasty, and Feng Dao lost the chance to sit for the imperial examination for the whole country had fallen into chaos. Feng

Dao had to go work for a feudal lord named Liu Shouguang so as to begin his political career.

Liu Shouguang was soon defeated by other feudal lords, and Feng Dao had to go work for yet another lord. Meanwhile, Feng Dao had won acclaim for his talent and his new master, Zhang Chengye, recommended him to King Jing, Li Cunmao, who later became Emperor Zhuangzong of the Later Tang of the Five Dynasties period. Feng Dao wrote most skillfully, so Li Cunmao appreciated his ability and granted him an official post at the Imperial Academy. When the Later Tang was established, Emperor Li Cunmao immediately appointed Feng Dao his prime minister. From that moment, Feng Dao set out on a distinguished career spanning ten emperors in four different dynasties.

According to the tenets of Confucianism, Feng Dao was thus both unfilial and disloyal. A woman should not marry two men, so how could a subject serve different masters in different dynasties? Let us put this thought aside, since serving ten emperors is apparently no easy task, let alone keeping them satisfied. But Feng Dao accomplished this. Let us see how and why he could.

As a scholar living in troubled times, Feng Dao, like many a commoner born to poverty, hated war and longed for peace. He suffered during the various wars and had to shift from one feudal lord to another for patronage. At the outset of his political career, Feng Dao had always insisted on his own opinion and advised his master in blunt terms. While serving the feudal lord Liu Shouguang, he was put into jail because he openly advised Liu not to attack another lord. Although he escaped death at the last moment, Feng Dao learned a great lesson from this episode.

Throughout his life, Feng Dao made peace his unswerving objective. At the same time, he paid great attention to skills of persuasion when influencing his masters to do something beneficial for peace.

When Qidan, a small ethnic group, occupied the Central Plain, the ruler asked Feng Dao, "How can the people be saved?"

Feng Dao replied: "Nobody, not even the Buddha, can save them except Your Majesty."

On the surface Feng Dao was flattering the emperor, but in fact he was hoping that the burning, killing and other ravages of war could be avoided. On hearing Feng Dao's words, the Qidan ruler was most glad and changed his original course of action. People in later generations commended the prime minister: "It is Feng Dao who helped the people of the Central Plain avert destruction by the Qidan."

Feng Dao spanned four dynasties and served ten different rulers, experiencing both commendation and censure many times over. Even if the ruler had changed, Feng Dao was unchanged in his mindset. Whenever he advised rulers or colleagues, he always made them feel comfortable and then offered his own opinions in diplomatic words. Through his unique efforts, many wars were avoided, yet at the same time he maintained his integrity.

Feng Dao holds a special place in Chinese history, and people of later generations have called him, "one who rolled through troubled times."

# Song Dynasty
# (960-1279)

# Sima Guang, Conservative in Politics and Reformer in Historiography

The tale of "Sima Guang Cracking the Jar" is still popular among Chinese children. It goes like this:

Long, long ago (to be exact, around 1025), when Sima Guang was still a small child, he was playing with some other children in a garden. One of them suddenly tumbled into a huge jar full of water. All the other children panicked, all of them that is, except Sima Guang. While the other children cried and screamed, Sima Guang picked up a stone and smashed the jar. As a result, the child who almost drowned in the jar was saved. The sharp-witted child, Sima Guang, later became prime minister of the Southern Song Dynasty and left future generations the great book *History as a Mirror*.

Born to an official family, Sima Guang (1019-1086) studied hard from the time he was small. It is said that he had read almost all the books then available by the time he was 15 years old. In the

year 1038, during the reign of Emperor Renzong, he passed the imperial examination, and set out on his political career.

From Emperor Renzong through Emperor Yingzong and Emperor Shenzong, Sima Guang's star kept rising. When Wang Anshi, during the reign of Emperor Shenzong, launched his well-known reforms, Sima Guang, representing the conservatives, was totally opposed. He was first demoted and eventually he submitted his resignation.

The relationship between Sima Guang and Wang Anshi was not a simple one. During the reign of Emperor Renzong, both men maintained a decent personal relationship, as they were eminent men of letters and had much in common—but they held different views on how to run a state. Wang Anshi thought reforms had to be carried out so as to eradicate certain social evils, such as unsound financial practices and insufficient national strength. From Sima Guang's point of view, running a state was something akin to running a house, extensive reconstruction was necessary only to avoid great danger. He did not think it was time for such changes. On the contrary, he advocated upholding the laws and regulations promulgated in the earlier Northern Song Dynasty. Sima

Guang wrote to Wang Anshi three times explaining his doubts about the intended reforms. As an upright man, he even warned Wang Anshi to be careful about certain villains surrounding him. Thus, even though both were politically opposed, there was no personal vendetta involved.

As a Confucian scholar, Sima Guang strongly adhered to Confucian belief in absolute loyalty to the ruler and the court. He often said: "I have received much from the state, I should return even more." He spoke his mind candidly whenever needed.

Once while Emperor Renzong was touring temples with his wife and concubines, they stopped to enjoy a performance at Xuande Gate. The program included topless women sumo wrestlers displaying their skills in an arena. According to Confucianism, women should not be allowed to appear in public, let alone appear in bikini-like clothing. When Sima Guang heard of this he immediately presented a report to the emperor. It read: "While the country is enduring various natural disasters, an emperor should not be enjoying such indecent performances." The emperor was certainly not thrilled to read his plaint, but this is not what concerned Sima Guang. Sima Guang knew it was his responsibility to tell the ruler what he thought was right.

As a high-ranking official, Sima Gang was quite self-restrained, living a very austere life. According to certain historical records, Sima Guang seldom ate meat or wore silk. During a time when aristocrats and officials pursued lives of luxury, Sima Guang was an exception to this rule. He did not care for any type of opulence. The following interesting anecdote should prove this.

When Sima Guang, at the age of 20, passed the imperial examination, scholars had to participate in a traditional ceremony. The emperor granted a corsage to each one to wear at the ceremony; Sima Guang, however, did not want to wear any such ornamentation, until one of his classmates warned him: "You cannot disobey the emperor's orders." Thus, Sima Guang was forced to wear the corsage. But it was said that when Sima Guang died, all he left behind was a bed and some books.

Once the emperor had bestowed countless treasures on Sima Guang, but he had donated all of them to his office. The common people showed great respect for Sima Guang, unlike the general host of corrupt and greedy officials. When Sima Guang died in 1086, people in the capital city mourned the highly esteemed prime minister by closing down all their businesses. Those outside the capital also put up images of Sima Guang on their walls, offering sacrifices to him when they had their evening meal. At one time the distribution of images of Sima Guang could not keep pace with the increasing demand.

As a statesman, Sima Guang was a conservative and an upright official; as a man of letters and as a historian, his contribution was even greater. The great book he left, *History as a Mirror,* almost became required reading for rulers of later dynasties. Today, the influence of the book still remains, on both historiography and social practices.

Sima Guang had made the decision, when he was young, to one day write a book for contemporary rulers to learn lessons from historical experience. In the year 1066, he presented eight volumes of the book to Emperor Yingzong, who then encouraged him to complete the work.

Of the early historical writings, such as the *Spring and Autumn Annals* and *Records of the Historian,* there were then already more than a thousand volumes all together. It would have been impossible for one person to read through all of them in a single lifetime. How could this problem be solved, and how could a book about all these writings be comprehensive enough? Sima Guang pondered this dilemma and found a solution to this through his own great work, which took him 19 years to complete.

Through 294 volumes, *History as a Mirror* covers from the 23rd year of King Weilie of the Zhou Dynasty (403 BC), to the 6th year of Emperor Shizong of the Later Zhou Dynasty (959 AD), the dynasty before the Northern Song Dynasty. It records events across 12 dynasties spanning a total of 1362 years. As a comprehensive history written in the style of the annals, *History as a Mirror* was an unprecedented work. It contains the ideas of all the various schools of thought, and is a valuable archive of historical information. Sima Guang provided his own definitive commentary on many important historical events and figures. He not only explained his political criteria for choosing who was virtuous, and praised the righteous and criticized the wrongdoers, but he also recorded other diverse critical opinions. Sima Guang had hoped rulers would learn from history as well as from the personalities in the book. Readers today may look on it both as a historical record as well as a literary work. With its comprehensive accounts and vivid descriptions of historical figures, *History as a Mirror* is an indispensable masterwork. A famous scholar of the Qing Dynasty, Wang Mingsheng, praised it highly: "Heaven and Earth have bestowed a book that no scholar can ignore."

Behind such a great work, there had to be a great author. As a brilliant man of extensive learning, Sima Guang always studied very hard. In order to write *History as a Mirror*, Sima Guang worked around the clock. He asked a craftsman to invent a round wooden pillow, which he called a "Pillow Alarm," in order to avoid oversleeping. Whenever he turned over in bed, the wooden pillow would fall to the ground—in this way Sima Guang would awake to continue his work.

The writing of *History as a Mirror* was such a major undertaking that it could not have been accomplished without the support of others. The book also provided Sima Guang a chance to display his organizational talents to the fullest. He employed some of the most famous historians of his time, and divided the labor among them according to their field of expertise. Under Sima Guang's leadership, the work was accomplished smoothly and efficiently. It was said that the draft manuscripts filled two large houses. People who have examined this material in detail have found no hasty or careless writing.

Sima Guang also wrote some other history books, most of them relating to his major opus. After the publication of *History as a Mirror*, many people specialized in the study of it, both the writing of treatises as well as the developing of theories about the work. A new field of study thus emerged in China, based solely on *History as a Mirror*. Sima Guang is therefore credited as having greatly advanced the development of Chinese historiography.

While Sima Guang is noted for his reform of the science of history, he is seen as a conservative in politics. Wang Anshi's reforms had promoted the development of the society (see the following chapter), but Sima Guang was strongly opposed to these reforms. When Emperor Shenzong, who championed Wang Anshi's reforms, was succeeded by Emperor Zhezong, the new ruler appointed Sima Guang as his prime minister. As soon as he took over the post, Sima Guang abolished all the regulations and laws promulgated by Wang Anshi. Nonetheless, he was an official with a fine reputation among the common people, as he was upright and honest in performing his official duties. At the same time, he devoted his life to writing that most invaluable book *History as a*

*Mirror,* which represents a turning point in Chinese historiography. It is perhaps for this reason that Sima Guang is remembered as a great historian more than as a prime minister.

# Wang Anshi, Illustrious Statesman and Man of Letters

High school pupils still have to study Wang Anshi's writings in their Chinese classes. In popular perceptions Wang Anshi is remembered more as a man of letters than as a statesman. He is also listed among the eight most famous writers of the Tang and Song dynasties, a period known for the greatness of its writers and poets.

Wang Anshi was a prolific writer, but only two anthologies of his work are still extant, and his concise yet powerful writing style may be compared with the modern US writer Ernest Hemingway. In Wang Anshi's writings one always encounters new ideas, for as the Chinese saying goes: "Writing mirrors the writer." And so it was with his political career as well, where Wang Anshi promulgated his new ideas in bold, broad strokes.

Born to an official's family, Wang Anshi was well educated. He passed the imperial examination with excellent marks, becoming a local governor at the county level. According to the Song Dynasty laws, Wang Anshi could request promotion after three years of local experience. Yet, he did not do that. On the contrary, he asked to remain as a local official at different places. In this way, he felt he would learn about the real conditions of the common people, and do something beneficial for them.

Although Wang Anshi was not promoted like his colleagues were, he earned a good reputation among both the common people and the court.

In the year 1067, Emperor Shenzong ascended the throne. Having heard of Wang Anshi's good name long ago, the emperor summoned him to the palace.

This was to be a most memorable meeting for both the emperor and Wang Anshi.

"What matters most in ruling a country?" asked Emperor Shenzong.

Wang Anshi replied: "We must devise new laws and policies instead of blindly following tradition. Moreover, we need capable people to implement these new laws."

Wang Anshi pointed out that inadequate national revenues were a result of not employing capable people who could resolve financial problems, the most important being not overburdening the common people with new taxes.

The emperor considered his advice most

reasonable, and appointed Wang Anshi the prime minister. Thus with the support of the emperor, Wang Anshi commenced his reforms in the following year.

Wang Anshi's broad reforms covered the civil service, agriculture, education, examination, finance, and military affairs. The focus of his reforms was the development of production and the strengthening of military power. He enacted a series of measures, including an Equitable Land Tax Measure, a Land Reclamation and Water Conservancy Act, an Exemption of Corvee Act, an Agricultural Loan Act, and a Trade and Barter Measure.

After 16 years of Wang Anshi's new laws being implemented, remarkable gains were achieved. More than 10,000 irrigation works were completed and several hundred thousand acres of fields were irrigated. As a result, the common people benefited, state revenues expanded, and national defense was strengthened.

Despite this, Wang Anshi's reforms adversely affected top bureaucrats and business people who had benefited from the old laws. These people joined together to reverse Wang Anshi's new laws. Among them were famous men of letters and politicians, well known in Chinese history, such as Sima Guang, Su Dongpo and his brother Su Zhe. His detractors went to great lengths to impede the implementation of the new laws and force Wang Anshi's resignation. Eventually, in fact, this campaign led to Wang Anshi's first resignation.

Although the emperor soon reinstated him, Wang Anshi now had to face an even more powerful opposition. The matter got even worse when some supporters of the reforms began to disagree with one another. The emperor heard about these conflicts and began to distrust Wang Anshi's reforms.

When Wang Anshi realized it was impossible for his reforms to succeed, he again submitted his resignation as prime minister, this time claiming poor health. The emperor agreed, and Wang Anshi, mentally and physically exhausted, quietly withdrew from the political stage.

Wang Anshi's new laws were still practiced for a few years after his resignation, but soon ended in failure when his powerful opponents came to the force. The Northern Song Dynasty lost its last chance at recovery and was eliminated by the State of Jin in 1126.

After Wang Anshi left the court, he retired to the suburbs of today's Nanjing for more than a decade. Wang Anshi had devoted everything to his reforms and now possessed neither money nor treasure. Unlike many retired high-ranking officials, he lived a life of near poverty. On sunny days, he liked to journey up to the mountains or sail a boat down to the city. If it was rainy, he would stay inside his house, which had no garden or walls around it. Since his son had died young, he had no other family members living with him. Once he was so seriously ill, he thought he would pass away, and he donated his house to a temple. However, he eventually recovered, and then had to rent another house.

It was a most memorable day in the seventh month of 1084, when Su Dongpo—who along with Wang Anshi is considered one of the eight most famous writers of the Tang and Song dynasties, and more importantly, one of Wang Anshi's main political enemies—came to visit the retired prime minister, on his way to take up office at Yuzhou.

Su Dongpo was supposed to have said to Wang Anshi: "Sir, I'm most humbled to meet you, the great prime minister, please forgive my bad manners."

At which Wang Anshi smiled and replied: "Was courtesy set up for people like you and me?"

The two men both laughed. They then rode their donkeys, traveling up to Mount Jiang and staying a few nights at the temple discussing poetry. After several happy days together, Su Dongpo was very reluctant to say goodbye to Wang Anshi. Upon return to his office, Su Dongpo wrote a poem about his encounter with Wang Anshi.

At one time, Su Dongpo had opposed Wang Anshi's new laws and been jailed. Then Wang Anshi had left the capital in retirement. Now they had become old friends again.

After Su Dongpo's visit, Wang Anshi had no other chances to meet any other old contemporaries. He died peacefully at the age of 65 in the year 1086.

# Cai Jing, Great Calligrapher, Bad Prime Minister

The four most famous calligraphers of the Song Dynasty are Su Dongpo, Huang Tingjian, Mi Pei and Cai Jing. Yet due to his terrible performance as prime minister, people of later generations expunged Cai Jing's name from the list of the top four calligraphers. Cai Xiang, another calligrapher, was installed in his place. Here is the story of what happened to Cai Jing, and why people detested him so much.

Cai Jing (1047-1126), a native of what is today's Fujian Province, was a successful candidate at the imperial examinations held in the third year of the reign of Emperor Shenzong of the Northern Song Dynasty. The early years of Cai Jing's political career were not smooth, as he had witnessed many ups and downs.

When Emperor Huizong ascended the throne, a eunuch named Tong Guan gained the emperor's favor and wielded great authority. Being a collector of invaluable calligraphy and art works, Tong Guan always asked his followers to collect masterpieces for him. Hearing of this, Cai Jing presented his own collection to Tong Guan. As a result, the delighted Tong Guan wrote a letter to the emperor. It read: "Your Majesty, I have discovered a great talent for the court. You should not keep him in an insignificant position for too long." Soon after that, Cai Jing was promoted, and in a few years became prime minister. After that, both Tong Guan and Cai Jing became the real powers running the country.

Emperor Huizong is also remembered as a great calligrapher in Chinese history. In this regard, he and Cai Jing had much in common. The emperor appreciated very much Cai Jing's mastery of calligraphy and literature. Thus, whenever other officials criticized Cai Jing for his misdeeds, the emperor always protected Cai Jing. Nevertheless, he was removed from the post of prime minister four times during his political career. Each time, however, Cai Jing was recalled. He was certainly skillful at winning the emperor's good graces. And since Emperor Huizong was clearly not a good ruler, both he and Cai Jing were well matched as emperor and prime minister.

During Cai Jing's career, the Song Dynasty court was so corrupt that the emperors had to enact some new laws and regulations in response. For many years, despite the change of emperors and the rise and fall of prime ministers, there was an ongoing debate and battle for and against new laws. To keep a steady position in such circumstances was not easy. Cai Jing, who was at least skillful at seeing which way the wind blew, certainly knew how to protect himself.

The moment Cai Jing held power in the court, he set up his friends and relatives in key positions and tried his hardest to defeat those with dissident ideas. According to historical records, Cai Jing often pinned the "undesirable" label on those dissidents and had their names inscribed in stone. Cai Jing then ordered that they could not live in the capital or even enter the capital without his permission.

In this way, Cai Jing turned the court into his own kingdom. He even publicly auctioned off official titles. His house became a market for peddling various positions. Since each position had a fixed price, people had to pay what was demanded of them.

Throughout his life, especially when he was at the peak of his power, Cai Jing lived a life of luxury, enjoying gourmet food and a large retinue of cooks and servants. There is a story about an official who bought as a concubine a former cook from Cai Jing's house. When the official asked her to prepare a steamed dumpling for him, the woman replied: "I don't know how!" Her husband did not believe her, and said: "Impossible! You were a cook in the prime minister's house." To which the woman had replied: "That may be so, but I was only the cook in charge of cutting onions."

Each year on Cai Jing's birthday, officials across the country would present a large number of presents to Cai Jing, the gifts being classified as "Birthday Items." In order to win Cai Jing's favor, every official tried to obtain the best gifts from their localities. In *Outlaws of the Marsh*, one of the four most famous classical novels in Chinese history, a tale is recounted about how seven gallants stole one of Cai Jing's "Birthday Items." This indicates how deeply the common people of the time hated Cai Jing's misdeeds.

With the money extorted from the people, Cai Jing built magnificent mansions for himself. At the same time, he convinced the emperor to also enjoy life as he did. He set up several organizations to entertain the imperial family. In order to build beautiful gardens for the emperor, Cai Jing asked officials in Suzhou and Hangzhou, two cities famous for their gardens, to ship the huge and special stones to the capital for rockeries to decorate those gardens. It was well known that local officials also robbed anything of value from common people's houses. A scenario soon emerged of a large fleet of ships going up and down the canal each day. People later commented that Cai Jing had drained the wealth of the country.

Cavorting in splendid palaces and beautiful gardens, the emperor, however, was most thrilled. He is supposed to have commented: "Prime Minister Cai is most loyal to me. As Emperor I am enjoying the very best."

What the life of the common people was like at the time can be easily imagined. The contradictions between the ruling class and the common people sharpened day by day. A folk song went thus: "By killing Tong Guan and Cai Jing, we people will see a better world." Peasant rebellions broke out sporadically. Meanwhile, the Jin, a kingdom established by a smaller ethnic group in northern China, launched several attacks on the declining Northern Song Dynasty.

In the year 1125, Emperor Huizong announced his abdication and his son became the new emperor. Cai Jing realized that people across the country hated him and decided it was time for him to flee. Many officials presented reports to the new Emperor asking him to punish six bad officials. There is no doubt that Cai Jing headed the list. In face of public anger, the emperor banished Cai Jing to a remote locality.

On his way to take up his new position, Cai Jing is said to have wanted to buy something to eat. But when people heard that it was Cai Jing who was asking for food, they refused to sell. In his carriage, Cai Jing sighed: "I never knew I had lost people's hearts so completely!"

Not long after he arrived at the place, Cai Jing died. His dead body was not covered until one of his followers buried it a few days later. On hearing the news, people regretted that Cai Jing had not been publicly executed.

As a great calligrapher and scholar, Cai Jing possessed the talent to become a good prime minister. But he misused his ability. As a result, his name was expunged from the list of the four greatest calligraphers of the Song Dynasty, and his transgressions led to the Northern Song's fall soon after his death.

# Qin Hui's Thousand-Year Evil Name

It's common to find a kind of fried food named *youtiao*, or *youzhagui* (deep-fried devils) as it is called in the south, in most cities and towns in China—a pair of long and slender dough sticks deep-fried in hot oil. *Youtiao* is so easily made and so delicious. It may be hard to imagine that these two sticks of dough represent two people, Prime Minister Qin Hui and his wife. Qin Hui's tale explains how this came about.

Qin Hui (1090-1155) was a native of the city of Jiangning, today's Nanjing. As a young scholar of promise, Qin Hui easily became a key official of the Song Dynasty. At that time, Northern Song had just fallen, two emperors and some imperial family members having been captured by the State of Jin. At the capital city of the Song Dynasty, Kaifeng (in today's Henan Province), it was announced that the former prime minister of the Song Dynasty, Zhang Bangchang, would be the new emperor.

The officials of the Song Dynasty decided to

oppose the new appointment and requested that a member of the former imperial family be appointed as the new emperor. They wrote a letter signing their names on it one after another. As a high-ranking official, Qin Hui had no choice but to take a clear stand. So with great reluctance, Qin Hui signed his name.

When the ruler of the State of Jin read the letter, he was very angry. He ordered all the signatories brought before him. Yet the Jin ruler soon bought Qin Hui over by using a mixture of threats and the promises of great gain. That was perhaps what Qin Hui had all along wanted anyway.

At the time, Zhao Gou, an imperial member of the Song Dynasty, had set up the Southern Song Dynasty in Lin'an (now Hangzhou). In other words, the Jin and the Southern Song had divided the country in two: the Jin in the north and the Song in the south. Jin decided that Qin Hui would be a perfect spy for them in the Southern Song court.

One morning in October 1130, Qin Hui and his wife together with several followers took a small boat to the territory of the Southern Song. When they disembarked at Zhaozhou, at what is now Shaoxing (Zhejiang Province), they were arrested by local troops. They were soon dispatched to the capital city Lin'an.

At the Song court, Qin Hui told the emperor and officials of the great perils he had faced escaping the Jin. He even shed tears when speaking of those moments of danger. Some believed him, while some had grave doubts about his story. After so many officials had been captured, they wondered, how could a frail scholar like Qin Hui escape? More strangely, how had he been able to run away with his wife and his servants in tow?

The emperor, however, believed Qin Hui and was even deeply moved by his story. He immediately placed Qin Hui in a high-ranking position.

After winning the emperor's trust, Qin Hui was not remiss in making a show of his loyalty. When the court started to praise those in the north who had steadily opposed Zhang Bangchang, Qin Hui jumped at the chance. He told others how he too had been against Zhang Bangchang's accession and advocated the cause of Zhao Gou, and how he had been the first person to sign his name on the letter. Many people were not aware of the truth and believed his self-serving words.

Even though the Jin had captured his father and elder brother, Zhao Gou actually had no ambitions outside of maintaining his position. To his selfish way of thinking, although the other half of the country was under the Jin's control, he could himself still be the emperor in the south—while, if he fought against the Jin, anything could happen. Even if his father and brother were rescued, there was no gain in that for himself. So when he heard what Qin Hui had to say, he was very happy. Qin Hui told him: "Your Majesty, we'd better sign a peace treaty with the Jin. This way, everyone will enjoy peace, both in the north and south."

In the year 1131, Zhao Gou appointed Qin Hui his prime minister. After that, Qin Hui was officially placed in charge of negotiations for peace with the Jin. With a spy placed as high as Qin Hui in the Southern Song court, the Jin ruler thought they could pursue their plans undisturbed, advancing step by step.

Firstly, they had Qin Hui advise Zhao Gou that the north should be placed under the protection of the Jin, while the Song would only rule the people of the south. Zhao Gou and many officials and generals were after all natives of the north, and felt they could not accept this advice. An outraged Zhao Gou had Qin Hui removed from office.

Jin's first tactic had failed, and so they

resorted to force.

Despite Jin's onslaught, some famous generals of the Southern Song such as Yue Fei and Han Shizhong were able to launch a powerful counterattack. Jin's military advantage was considerably weakened.

One of his officials advised the Jin ruler: "The balance of power is shifting. We had better pursue another strategy. The best course is to sign a peace treaty with the Song." The Jin ruler gave his approval.

Hearing the news, Zhao Gou thought the peace he had sought for years had arrived at long last. He re-appointed Qin Hui his prime minister, and put him in charge of all peace negotiations once again.

Qin Hui, wielding real power in his hands once more, made every effort to pursue peace negotiations. He realized, however, that there were obstacles in the way. Firstly, most common people did not want to make peace at a time when the military balance favored the Song. Then there were the troops that had just won significant victories. Qin Hui, though not afraid of the common people, had to deal with the army.

At that time, Zhang Jun, Han Shizhong and

Yue Fei were the generals in charge of Song's military. In order to undermine their power, Qin Hui hatched a plot.

One day Qin Hui, in the name of Zhao Gou, called them before the court. He asked them: "It seems that the emperor is tired of war after years of fighting. Generals, do you have any good ideas of how and when we will end our war with the Jin?" Believing that Qin Hui and the emperor really wanted an honest answer, each of them aired their own opinions.

Hearing their words, Qin Hui nodded and said: "Well, the emperor will be glad to know this, and I promise you will all be promoted."

The following day, the three generals were then actually promoted but to higher civilian positions. Qin Hui asked the emperor to postpone the announcement, so the three generals had to stay in the court for another two days.

Qin Hui then ordered his followers to replace the three generals at their military posts and remove their men from the army. Zhang, Han and Yue had no idea what was going on with the army. After several days, having heard no news from Qin Hui, they decided to visit him, saying: "Sir, it's time for us to return to the frontline. Do you have anything to announce?"

Qin Hui replied: "Congratulations! The three of you are all promoted to higher civilian positions. Also, you need not return to the frontline, for you are not generals anymore."

They thus discovered Qin Hui's plot, but it was already too late.

Yue Fei was the general the Jin troops feared most. The Jin ruler ordered Qin Hui to kill Yue Fei and his son, Yue Yun, who was also a brave general, as quickly as possible.

Qin Hui decided to consistently denounce Yue Fei to the Song emperor. He told the emperor: "Yue Fei does not want peace. His aim is to overwhelm the Jin and reinstate the two former emperors." Zhao Gou grew afraid on hearing this. If the two former emperors were returned to power, it would be impossible for him to remain emperor of the Song. He therefore conspired with Qin Hui to eliminate Yue Fei and his son. Thus Yue Fei, a patriotic general most famous in Chinese history, was secretly killed by Qin Hui.

After Qin Hui had removed the obstacles to his "peace negotiations" with the Jin, an agreement was soon signed. The Song became an attachment to the State of Jin, while the latter acknowledged the former's existence as long as it was limited to a certain territory. As well, the Song had to present a large quantity of treasures and silks to the Jin every year. This no doubt added greater burdens on the common people.

Zhao Gou and Qin Hui, however, were most satisfied with the result: Zhao Gou could still be the emperor of the Song, while his father and brother were held prisoner in the State of Jin; Qin Hui continued as prime minister, holding the real reins of power in the Song court. But this Song had no resemblance to the former power; it possessed less than half the territory of the Northern Song, and more importantly, it was now subservient to the State of Jin.

Later, in memory of the murdered General Yu Fei, the people built a temple, the Yue Fei Tomb, which can be found in present-day Hangzhou. In order to express their hatred for Qin Hui, they also made two figures out of dough to represent Qin Hui and his wife forever kneeling down before an image of Yue Fei. Made of dough into a snack called *youtiao* or *youzhagui*, this grew to become a most widespread symbol. Thus, these two sticks of dough representing Prime Minister Qin Hui and his wife have been fried in hot oil for people's breakfast almost every day for the past nearly one thousand years.

Retaining the post of prime minister for 19

years, Qin Hui died in his bed. Yet, he has had to bear the burden of an evil name long, long after his death.

# Yuan Dynasty
# (1271-1368)

# Yelü Chucai, Distinguished Statesman from the Qidan

Throughout China's long history, there have been several hundred emperors, but only one ever gained worldwide prominence. This of course is no other than Genghis Khan, the great Mongolian emperor and conqueror. At the time of Genghis Khan's ascendancy, China was divided into several parts. In the south, the Southern Song maintained its rule over the Han people; in the Central Plain, the State of Jin had established a new regime after the fall of the Northern Song Dynasty; meanwhile to the north of Beijing, the Mongolians grew stronger and stronger. Yelü Chucai (1190-1244), a Qidan, was a scion of the Liao imperial family. Liao, a state established by the Qidan people in what is now northeast China, was eliminated by the State of Jin in the year 1200. Yelü Chucai's father then served at Jin's court. When Yelü Chucai was old enough, he was selected, due to his great ability, as a prefectural official.

In the year 1214, as Genghis Khan's troops

marched on Beijing, the State of Jin moved its capital from Beijing to Kaifeng (in present-day Henan Province). Yelü Chucai was left to guard Beijing, then known as Zhongdu. With his intrepid Mongolian troops, Ghengis Khan soon occupied Zhongdu. Hearing of Yelü Chucai's name, Ghengis Khan asked to meet him. He told Yelü Chucai: "Liao and Jin have been enemies for several generations. What would you think if I took revenge on your behalf?"

"My grandfather and father were both officials of the State of Jin. How dare I regard my ruler as my enemy?" Yelü Chucai is said to have replied.

Genghis Khan, pleased with his answer, had Yelü Chucai stay with him. After that, Yelü Chucai had the chance to bring his talents into full play.

In the year 1227, Genghis Khan died. The Great Khan had four sons and they were all heirs to the throne. At councils to choose a new ruler, the decision was repeatedly deferred. Yelü Chucai knew that the longer the issue remained unresolved, the worse the situation would become. When Genghis Khan was alive, he had often spoken of selecting his third son Ogdai as his successor, though he never formally announced it. Yelü Chucai then told the second son of Genghis Khan: "Your father wanted your brother Ogdai to be the new ruler. Although you are Ogdai's elder brother, your duty would be to obey his will. If you kneel down before Ogdai and acknowledge his claim, who else would dare disagree? We must decide on a new ruler as soon as possible, or the consequences may be unimaginable." The second prince is said to have then knelt down before his young brother Ogdai and acclaimed him as the new ruler. In this way, the issue of succession was resolved and conditions stabilized. After this, the ruler and the second prince both honored Yelü Chucai, telling him: "You are truly the country's guiding star!"

For more than twenty years, Yelü Chucai made great contributions to the Mongolian kingdom, first having followed Genghis Khan then Ogdai hither and thither. Wherever he found himself, as a scholar and a man of letters, Yelü Chucai never stopped reading and writing. Today, we have his collected works in 14 volumes, including more than 600 poems. He was the only poet who saw firsthand how the great Genghis Khan set out to conquer the west. On this point alone, his poems were invaluable.

The Mongolians were nomads who lived on horseback and paid little attention to agricultural production. Stressing "Confucian government," Yelü Chucai devoted himself to changing their nomadic lifestyle and to developing agricultural production. Once a Mongolian autocrat had advised Genghis Khan that he better kill or drive the Han people away, turning their fields into pastures. Yelü Chucai disagreed and told Genghis Khan: "Your Majesty, you need supplies for your troops. Why not exercise a benevolent policy toward the Han people and ask them to provide supplies for our troops? This will make both sides happy." When the country's granaries were filled, Genghis Khan was most happy indeed. Due to Yelü Chucai's counsel, many Han lives were saved and people's lives became comparatively stable. Due to his efforts, the economy developed and the wounds of war were healed.

Yelü Chucai, who was from the Qidan minority people in China, was a great statesman, as well as a man of letters, who has carved himself a special place in Chinese history.

# Ming Dynasty
(1368-1644)

# Shi Kefa, a Loyal Prime Minister to a Doomed Dynasty

In the later years of the Ming Dynasty, the people had to endure a corrupt and decadent government. It was in such circumstances that Shi Kefa (1602-1645), who was to become the Southern Ming's prime minister and be known as a hero of the Han people, was born in what is today a suburb of Beijing.

At age 27, Shi Kefa passed the imperial examination and started out on his political career. Born to an official's family, Shi Kefa observed keenly how his grandfather and father performed their duties. As an incorruptible official, upon retirement Shi's grandfather came home with nothing.

Shi Kefa's grandfather was his best teacher. He taught the young man not only literature but also martial arts—and most importantly, the way to remain an honest and capable official. Shi Kefa, setting out on his political career after passing the imperial examination, was determined to follow his grandfather's teachings.

After a few years, Shi Kefa became a high-ranking general in the Ming army. Once during a cold winter, Shi Kefa and his troops had to fight in southern China, while keeping their horses running day and night, with no proper place to rest. Sharing the hardships of the soldiers, Shi Kefa is said to have slept on the frosted grassland and eaten the same food as his men.

"He cares for his subjects as if they were his own children." In ancient China, this is the highest praise an official could hear from the common people. Shi Kefa was such an official. Once a subordinate named Su killed an old woman over some petty matter. On hearing this, Shi Kefa was so angry that he sentenced the official to death. A few of this official's friends were against Shi Kefa's decision and incited rebellion.

When the rebel soldiers rushed into Shi Kefa's tent, they found him sitting in the center, wearing his general's uniform, looking calm and stern. Even before Shi Kefa had heard the news of the rebellion, he had already ordered other subordinates to depart, taking with them all the important documents. This prudent action really surprised the rebel soldiers. In ancient Chinese culture, generally speaking, the higher one's position was, the lesser the danger, so the more secure and arrogant higher officials tended to be. Shi Kefa's awe-inspiring posture shocked these soldiers, and they fell into a panic and ran away.

Chongzhen, the last emperor of the Ming Dynasty, had long heard of Shi Kefa's reputation for righteousness and honesty, but did not believe it. He sent several eunuchs to secretly investigate him. When these eunuchs learned that Shi Kefa was on the way to his hometown in Zhuozhou (in present-day Hebei Province), they decided to lay in wait on the only road through which he had to pass. As soon as Shi Kefa arrived, they stopped him and examined his luggage. According to Chinese custom, returning to one's hometown is an important event. As the saying goes: "Return home after making good." Generally, people liked to return home with lots of cash and the best clothes. These eunuchs found that Shi Kefa was not a typical returnee. Among Shi Kefa's luggage, they found several fans, reports to the emperor and some small change. There was nothing of value to be found. On hearing this, the emperor sighed: "There are few officials like Shi Kefa!"

In the year 1639, Shi Kefa's father died. According to custom, a man must mourn his dead parents for three years at home no matter what his situation. When his subordinates heard the news, they all came to see Shi Kefa off. Some even cried and stood in front of his horse, for they were afraid Shi Kefa would not return.

In the year 1644, the peasant army led by Li Zicheng occupied Beijing and Emperor Chongzhen was forced to commit suicide at what is now called Jingshan Park. Thus, the Ming Dynasty met its end. In May of the same year, a prince of the Ming imperial family, Zhu Yousong, declared himself Emperor in the city now known as Nanjing. His small court has been called in Chinese history the Southern Ming. Zhu Yousong appointed Shi Kefa prime minister. By this time, Manchu troops had forced Li Zicheng to abandon Beijing and established the Qing Dynasty.

The Southern Ming court meanwhile only occupied the eastern part of the Yangtze River valley and faced imminent peril from Qing troops who could invade at any time. Even under such circumstances, some officials still wasted time engaging in court infighting. Shi Kefa was so loyal to the Ming that he asked to fight at the frontline in the city of Yangzhou.

The prince regent of the Qing Dynasty, Dorgon (see next chapter) wrote to Shi Kefa, advising him to surrender to the Qing court as other Ming generals had done. Shi Kefa refused and wrote a letter in response, which read: "I have decided to give my life to help restore the Ming Dynasty!"

On the surface, the Ming Dynasty had fallen due to attacks by peasant rebels and Qing troops—when in fact its own cruel and corrupt government had been its downfall. It was to such a court that Shi Kefa was loyal, thus sealing his fate. For even in this small Southern Ming court, some officials continued to jockey for power at this most critical moment.

Shi Kefa, a loyal subject to the Ming, had to fight single-handedly against the Qing troops. Other than a few of his followers, no other officials supported him. Some even quickly surrendered to the Qing when the cities they were guarding were attacked by Qing troops.

By this time, Yangzhou was a city under siege, surrounded by the Qing army. Shi Kefa knew the situation was hopeless. He wrote these last words: "I was born at the wrong time and thus was not able to realize my ideals. It is my duty to die for the state." When the Qing troops sent an envoy to convince Shi Kefa to surrender, Shi Kefa refused, saying: "There will be no surrender from the prime minister of the Ming Dynasty. I will die with the city." Two of his subordinates wanted to kidnap Shi Kefa in order to surrender to the Qing. When Shi Kefa discovered this, he told them: "You do as you please for yourselves." The two men fled over to the Qing camp.

Inspired by Shi Kefa's determination, the remaining soldiers held on steadfastly in Yangzhou, fighting bravely against the Qing troops. Before the battle of Yangzhou, the Qing troops had never encountered such indomitable resistance. Nonetheless, given such a marked imbalance in strength, Yangzhou was finally occupied by the Qing army.

Although Shi Kefa was killed, even his enemy was moved by his heroism. One of Shi Kefa's followers built a cenotaph in memory of Shi Kefa at the foot of Mount Plum-Blossom outside of the city of Yangzhou.

As this prime minister was willing to die for his state and his nation, people of later generations still hold him in great respect. His opus, *The Work of Shi Zhongzheng* (another name by which he is known), is still read by people in China today.

# Qing Dynasty
# (1644-1911)

# Dorgon, the Iron-handed Prince Regent

The last feudal dynasty in China, the Qing Dynasty, was built by the Manchus. The original Manchu people lived in the northeast of China, outside of Shanhai Pass. Later, their ruler Nuerhachi established the powerful state of Qing. When peasant rebels almost eliminated the Ming Dynasty, the Qing emperor at the time, Huangtaiji, son of Nuerhachi, seized the opportunity and, after routing the peasant army, occupied the capital Beijing. However, just before the Qing troops entered Beijing, Huangtaiji fell seriously ill. Huangtaiji called his consanguineous brother Dorgon to his bed and asked him to look after Shunzhi his youngest son —who was only six years old—as well as his mother, the empress. And most importantly, Huangtaiji asked his brother to realize his dream of unifying the whole of China and building a new empire.

As the most trusted brother of Huangtaiji, Dorgon would in fact have been the most competent successor to the throne after Huangtaiji. Among Nuerhachi's 16 sons, Dorgon and his two brothers had been born to the same mother, Nuerhachi's cleverest and most beautiful concubine. The second son of Nuerhachi, Daishan, was afraid that this woman and her three sons would be a threat to him in the future and forced Dorgon's mother to commit suicide.

When Huangtaiji, the fourth son of Nuerhachi, had ascended the throne he was very generous to Dorgon and his two brothers. This kindness made Dorgon most loyal to him. Throughout many wars, Dorgon was always the first one to brave the thrusts of enemy spears, throwing his all into the fight. At the same time, Huangtaiji responded to Dorgon's loyalty in kind. Dorgon was not only his most beloved brother but also the highest-ranking prince among all the sons of Nuerhachi.

In the year 1643, one year before the Qing's march into Beijing, Huangtaiji died. Since the Manchus had been nomadic people before they established the Qing Dynasty, they had their own method of deciding a successor to the throne, when the seat of rule was far from the Shanhai Pass. During dynasties before the Qing, the emperor had been the only person who could decide who would be the next ruler. Yet with the

Manchu people, all imperial family members and high-ranking officials would come to discuss together this issue of succession. At the time, aside from Dorgon, another man Haoge, Huangtaiji's eldest son, was also a powerful contender to the throne. They each had officials and troops to support them. If either of them had declared themselves the new emperor, war would have broken out. In such a situation, Dorgon made a surprising move: he decided that the youngest son of Huangtaiji, Shunzhi, should be the new ruler. There were three reasons for Dorgon to do this: first, Shunzhi was Huangtaiji's most beloved son; second, Shunzhi's mother was Huangtaiji's favorite concubine, smart and beautiful; third, this was the only way to smooth the conflict between the two sides and resolve the problem. Certainly, Haoge was taken by surprise by Dorgon's suggestion. After a long silence, everyone agreed. Dorgon even ordered the death of two men who put forward the idea that he should be the emperor. As a result, the imminent outbreak of war was averted. And more importantly, the Qing could focus on the goal of unifying the whole of China.

On August 26, 1643, the six-year-old Shunzhi ascended the Qing throne and appointed Dorgon and his cousin Jierhalang the princes regent.

As an ambitious man, Dorgon certainly could not resign himself to handling state affairs along with others, including his opponent Haoge, or for that matter, with Jierhalang who shared his same position, as well as with the many other princes. Thus the next step for Dorgon was to rise above all others except the emperor. Since the emperor was still a child, Dorgon aspired to hold the real strings of power in the court.

Several months later, Dorgon announced that the process by which princes of all ranks together discussed state affairs should be abolished due to its inefficiency. Instead, the two princes regent alone should have the right to decision-making. Moreover, reports to the emperor had to be sent first to Dorgon.

As for his political opponent, Haoge, Dorgon certainly could not ignore him. In 1644, accused of conspiracy against the state, Haoge was arrested and his followers were put to death. Due to the emperor's intercession, Haoge escaped death but lost his power forever.

Throughout the following several months, Dorgon eliminated his enemies and became the real power in the Qing court.

In March 1644, the peasant army under Li Zicheng occupied Beijing, forcing the last emperor of the Ming Dynasty, Chongzhen, to commit suicide on Mount Jingshan. Before even hearing this news, Dorgon had already known that the days of the Ming Dynasty were numbered. He saw it as a great opportunity to unite China, and thus marched toward Shanhai Pass, the sole gateway to the Central Plain.

The general guarding Shanhai Pass, Wu Sangui, was a very famous Ming general. At first, he had wanted to surrender to the peasant rebels, but when he heard that Li Zicheng had ill-treated his family in Beijing, he changed his mind. This was a turning point both for Li Zicheng and the Qing.

Dorgon was certainly delighted when Wu Sangui opened the gates of Shanhai Pass to welcome him. Wu Sangui told him that the emperor of the Ming had died and Li Zicheng had occupied Beijing, the capital city of the Ming Dynasty.

On hearing the news, Dorgon became so excited he ordered an immediate attack on Beijing. Although Li Zicheng had been the first to arrive in Beijing, Wu Sangui's surrender to the Qing delivered him a fatal blow. The outer gate to Beijing had been opened. Furthermore, Li Zicheng did not act in time. He and his generals were eager to fight for position, treasure and beautiful women, instead of strengthening their regime. That was why Dorgon had easily eliminated Li Zicheng in a few days.

On May 2 in the year 1644, the Qing army entered Beijing, turning a new page in history. The last feudal dynasty in Chinese history, the Qing Dynasty, was established, and Shunzhi became the emperor of the Qing.

At the beginning of the Qing Dynasty, the conflicts among different classes and ethnic groups were intense and complex. The Manchus were a smaller ethnic group mainly living north of the Shanhai Pass, while the Han people, who had lived in central China for centuries, were used to being ruled by regimes established by Han emperors. A strong opposition against the Qing Dynasty arose across the whole country.

Under such pressures, Dorgon wisely undertook a series of measures. First, he steadily carried on the fight to unify the whole of China. He sent troops to wipe out Li Zicheng as well as the imperial members of the former Ming Dynasty who had fled. After a few years, most of China was under the control of the Qing court. On the other hand, he helped to organize the ruling structures at all levels. Since the Manchus were mainly nomadic people before it established the Qing, it was impossible for them to make use of their limited tradition and culture to rule a people of a more complex society. Dorgon knew this clearly. On the basis of Ming laws, he instituted the promulgation of the Qing's laws and regulations. To those former Ming officials and generals who wanted to serve the Qing court, he granted them proper positions. He made Wu Sangui an exemplary model and gave him a title even higher than what he had received in the Ming Dynasty. Dorgon also advocated Confucianism, the ruling ideology of the Han people, and therefore achieved much progress through this policy. A great number of feudal lords in northern China surrendered to the Qing government. Thus it was not too long before they established their rule over the areas they had occupied.

Certainly, Dorgon did not forget that the Manchus were the ruling ethnic group who would see themselves as superior to others. With his agreement, Manchu aristocrats and officials occupied a large quantity of the most fertile fields of the Han people. As a result, numerous Han people lost their own lands, becoming the slaves of the Manchu aristocracy. The other decree made by Dorgon was that all Han males had to wear long queues like Manchu men did. According to Han custom, only women plaited their hair while men had short hair. This was clearly seen as a humiliation of Han males. Rebellions on a small scale against the Qing Dynasty rose and fell here and there, throughout the first fifty years of the Qing.

During the first seven years after the establishment of the Qing Dynasty, Dorgon was the real ruler of the country while the child emperor Shunzhi was only a puppet. Dorgon enjoyed the power of an emperor and lived the life of an emperor too. He built magnificent palaces and beautiful parks for himself. He even placed the emperor's imperial stamp in his own house. Dorgon even married the emperor's mother, the Dowager Xiaozhuangwen. This would not have happened with any imperial family of any other dynasty. According to Confucian tradition, a woman may have only one husband throughout her life, even if the husband fell dead at the wedding. But the Manchus were a nomadic people before they established the Qing Dynasty, and still retained some of their customs in the early years of their rule. No historical records give the reasons why the beautiful and clever dowager married Dorgon. Did they love each other? Or did the dowager and her son need Dorgon's protection? No one knows. This is an exception in Chinese history, where a dowager married a subject who was also her brother-in-law. It seems, however, that Dorgon was not faithful to his exceptional wife, and their marriage was said to be an unhappy one.

In November 1650, while Dorgon was hunting outside Beijing, he fell seriously ill. On the way back, he fell to the ground from his horse. This further worsened his condition. That December of the same year, Dorgon died in a small city at the foot of the Great Wall. He was only 39 years old.

After Dorgon's death, his name retained neither power nor honorable title. Those who hated him and were against him finally had their opportunity. Two months after Dorgon's death, his opponents presented a petition to the emperor. It read: "Dorgon wanted to replace Your Majesty, therefore he and his family must be seriously punished." Not long after that, Emperor Shunzhi ordered the confiscation of Dorgon's titles and the destruction of his tomb. Many of his followers were killed and expelled from their offices. Only after the fourth emperor of the Qing Dynasty, Emperor Qianlong, ascended the throne, was Dorgon rehabilitated and his offspring granted high-ranking titles.

As the true founder of the Qing Dynasty, Dorgon made a great contribution to the unification of China. But he obviously enjoyed too much power as a subject of the real emperor, thus he suffered the ignominy of being whipped after his death.

# He Shen, the Most Corrupt Prime Minister in Chinese History

Not far from the beautiful Beihai Park in Beijing, there is an exquisite construction with a large garden, the Mansion of Prince Gong. This house once belonged to He Shen, a prime minister of Emperor Qianlong in the mid Qing Dynasty. Although not as huge and as luxurious as an imperial palace, this house is the finest official residence to be found in China.

Born to an aristocratic Manchu family, He Shen (1750-1799) received a good education at home when he was a child. Later, he and his brother were sent to study at the Imperial School in the palace. The Imperial School was a training ground for the mandarins of the future.

It was said that He Shen was handsome and clever. In the Imperial School, he was educated in a rigorous and comprehensive way. In addition to history as well as languages including Manchu, Mongolian and Mandarin Chinese, he had to learn many other arts, such as horsemanship, archery and marksmanship. He Shen had an extraordinary memory and studied most diligently, and his teachers were said to have always praised him highly. After several years of study, he had mastered several languages and could recite by heart The Four Books *(The Great Learning, The Doctrine of the Mean, The Analects of Confucius,* and *The Books of Mencius)* as well as The Five Classics *(The Book of Songs, The Book of History, The Book of Changes, The Book of Rites,* and *The Spring and Autumn Annals)*. Furthermore, his calligraphy and artwork were exquisite.

Like most scholars, He Shen wanted to gain eminence via the imperial examination. Yet, he failed in the following year's examination. Two years later, however, he received another chance, and was selected as an imperial bodyguard. This was not a high position, yet it became much easier for He Shen to approach the emperor.

One day, while Emperor Qianlong was reciting *The Analects of Confucius* in his carriage, he forgot one of the lines and asked his followers: no one but He Shen could tell him. The emperor noticed that He Shen was young, handsome and elegant, and he began to regard He Shen with a certain admiration. This small incident helped turn a new leaf in He Shen's life.

Within the span of only a year, He Shen was promoted several times. At age 27, He Shen became one of the emperor's prime ministers and was deeply involved in making important decisionss. Later, the emperor allowed his beloved daughter to marry He Shen's eldest son. Now, as a relative of the imperial family, the emperor's confidence in He Shen deepened.

Yet, though He Shen possessed the capabilities to be a good prime minister, he did not make use of his talents on behalf of the nation. He only conccentrated on how to win the emperor's favor and accumulate his own wealth.

He learned everything about the emperor, such as his temperament, his habits and his manners. He Shen could figure out not only what the emperor was thinking about, he also knew what the emperor could not do. Here are some examples.

Qianlong liked to write poems, and in Chinese history he became the emperor credited with writing the most poems. In order to please the emperor, He Shen also wrote many poems to show to the emperor.

As the emperor liked traveling, He Shen always accompanied him on his many visits out of the capital.

Qianlong was also an avid collector. He Shen always did his best to collect rare treasures to please the emperor. Once He Shen delighted Qianlong by presenting the emperor with a large gold Buddha as a birthday gift.

Although He Shen was the prime minister and the highest-ranking mandarin, as well as the father-in-law of the princess, whenever the emperor spat, he would hold the royal spittoon in both hands, to be of service.

The emperor also responded in kind to He Shen's ministrations. He trusted He Shen more than he did his own sons. This in turn made the emperor's sons and grandsons most afraid of He Shen.

In the late years of Qianlong's reign, He Shen was the most powerful mandarin in the court. He held supreme power in all affairs—political, financial and military. After he was promoted to first place among all officials, He Shen instituted reforms in politica; and cultural affairs. He utilized his reforms to make use of anyone he liked and push out those who were against him.

From his unique position of power, it was easy for He Shen to accumulate wealth. For, in order to curry favor with He Shen, many people bribed him. A huge web of corruption was spun out, with He Shen at its core.

Corruption and bribery became widespread all over the country. Although the emperor was aware of it and punished some corrupt officials, he fiercely protected He Shen. Therefore the emperor was ultimately to be blamed.

Under the protection of the emperor, He Shen could get anything he wanted. He possessed vast stretches of land in several locales, especially in today's Beijing, Tianjin and Hebei Province. It was said that He Shen's houses could be found in every district of Beijing. Other than owning property, He Shen also ran several other businesses, such as local banks, pawnshops, groceries, hotels, restaurants and antique shops. He almost monopolized the market.

He Shen, possessing the wealth of a king, certainly lived a very opulent life. After growing tired of all kinds of expensive delicacies, he even took to eating a large fresh pearl everyday. He also liked to wear fashionable clothing. It was said that the buttons of one of his robes were all made of small Western-style clocks. This was certainly very rare two hundred years ago, and even today the value of his finery would be priceless. He hired many servants to work for him and his large number of wives. Still he was very stingy with his servants. They never got to eat their fill, and had no right to pocket money.

In the 60th year of his reign, Emperor Qianlong publicly announced that he would abdicate the following year and hand over the crown to one of his sons, Yongyan. When the new emperor, known as Jiaqing, ascended the throne, Qianlong still remained the real master of the country, and He Shen continued to be the first official among all others.

As Qianglong grew older, he came to depend only more and more on He Shen. Sometimes when Qianlong's writing was not clear, He Shen would tear the sheet to pieces, and write it himself. It was said that He Shen often gave orders to the new emperor in the name of Qianlong. Even foreigners were aware that He Shen, the prime minister, was the real power in the country.

However, He Shen's days of favor were numbered. In the fourth year of Emperor Jiaqing, Qianlong died suddenly during an illness. Emperor Jiaqing immediately arrested He Shen and threw him into jail. His tremendous wealth was confiscated. Not long after this, the emperor ordered He Shen to commit suicide. The most corrupt prime minister in Chinese history thus ended his life in a most unforeseen way.

## 图书在版编目（CIP）数据

中国古代宰相故事/程宇主编. —北京： 外文出版社，2001.10
ISBN 7-119-02917-7

I. 中... II. 程... III. 英语—语言读物，故事
IV. H319.4: I
中国版本图书馆 CIP 数据核字(2001)第 067077 号

责任编辑　梁良兴　程宇
封面设计　王志
插图绘制　李士伋

外文出版社网页：
http://www.flp.com.cn
外文出版社电子邮件地址：
info@flp.com.cn
sales@flp.com.cn

### 中国古代宰相故事

程宇　主编

\*

©外文出版社
外文出版社出版
(中国北京百万庄大街 24 号)
邮政编码　100037
通县大中印刷厂印刷
中国国际图书贸易总公司发行
(中国北京车公庄西路 35 号)
北京邮政信箱第 399 号　邮政编码 100044
2001 年(36 开)第 1 版
2001 年第 1 版第 1 次印刷
(英)
ISBN 7-119-02917-7/I・709 (外)
03500(平)
10-E-3473P